Make 2018 Great!
Anthony M. Flynn

THE HAPPINESS MAP

Finding Fulfillment in Work and Life

Dr. Emily Shupert & Anthony M. Flynn

with Bill Blankschaen

The Happiness Map: Finding Fulfillment in Work and Life

ISBN: 978-0-692-06148-0 (print)

First edition.

Printed in the U.S.A.

Created in partnership with Bill Blankschaen and his StoryBuilders team. (MyStoryBuilders.com)

Cover design by StoryBuilders.

Emily: To my mom and dad who dedicated their lives to the betterment of mine. I am forever grateful and changed by your endless and selfless love. Thank you!

Anthony: This book is dedicated to my amazing wife and children: Nikita, Taji and Alaya. You are my pride and joy. I am so grateful to have each of you in my life. I cannot imagine life without either of you and I am humbled by the fact that God chose me to do life with each of you. I look forward to many great years ahead as we all continue to fulfill our calling on earth!

CONTENTS

WHEN WILL I
BE HAPPY?

"Your problem is how you are going to spend this one odd and precious life you have been issued. Whether you're going to spend it trying to look good and creating the illusion that you have power over people and circumstances, or whether you are going to taste it, enjoy it and find out the truth about who you are."

—*Anne Lamott*

· ·

BIG IDEA
How do you
define happiness?

· ·

This book will *not* make you happy.

That's an odd way to start a book about happiness, don't you think? We agree. Before we can begin to support your journey toward finding happiness, we must first address a major problem—the shortage of practical resources and tools to help you become happier.

Don't get us wrong; we've read countless books and articles on the subject. Yet if you're like us and most Americans, you're left less happy and even more dissatisfied after reading *"happiness literature."* In fact, one study revealed that people who put greater emphases on getting happier *actually* become less happy, less satisfied, and have 75% more depressive symptoms.[1]

Whew! For all the happiness books, self-help programs, professional coaches, and even college degrees focused on this topic, those are sobering statistics. So why do most happiness books fall flat? Let's look at some of the reasons. Some authors offer cerebral theories from the perspective of privileged academics. These authors conduct limited studies with small sample sizes and announce their "findings" that don't always account for gender, socioeconomic status, race, etc. These findings make for interesting chatter at a cocktail party: "Did you know happier people have more meaningful friendships, are more satisfied in their romantic relationships, have better immune systems, sleep better, are more altruistic, are more liked by others, find greater meaning, and win the lottery more often?" (We're just kidding about the lottery bit, but it's not too far off.)

Candidly, we don't need a study to prove that someone who has satisfying relationships probably also has a greater sense of meaning in life. It only makes sense that they love their well-loved life, and, as a result, they're probably happier. They have a healthier lens through which they see the world. You could say these lucky few are the *optimistically privileged* because they can look at life and all its challenges through a mindset that is naturally more resilient and optimistic. We'd all love to see life through that lens, but knowing such people exist doesn't help us. In fact, it does the opposite. What we need to know is *how* to get there—*for the rest of us.*

Other books read more like personal journals from someone who has a specific process for life fulfillment that just can't work for most other people. Some of these people leave their corporate desk jobs behind for yearlong adventures deep in the Amazon rain forests. Others chase spiritual gurus to the heights of the Himalayas, in the vineyards of Tuscany, and in remote beaches of Indonesia. All claim to have had an epiphany—an "aha" moment they now publicize in a "one-size-fits-all" happiness manual for the masses. It feels empty to us; especially when the masses must keep their day jobs, raise their kids, and battle racial injustice and other evils in the world. Although we applaud their progress from information to application, their recommended process is all too often limited to their own perspectives and personal journeys.

Then there are the books so dense with neuropsychological terminology that even a psychology professional could get lost in the data. One outcome we don't want is for you to feel less intelligent and happy when you're done. True, we haven't done clinical research on thousands of study participants.

WE WON'T IGNORE THE DATA THAT'S OUT THERE, AS YOU'LL SEE, BUT IF ACADEMIC PEDIGREES OR EXHAUSTIVE RESEARCH PRODUCED HAPPINESS, NO ONE WOULD NEED THIS BOOK

So what makes this book any different? Why do we think you *need* to read this book? We've already said that this *book* won't make you happy. It's not a magical elixir. There are no pages that magically transport you to another place with unicorns and rainbows, endless golf courses, or whatever your personal version of utopia might be. However, what we have to offer really works! What we offer in this book is a simple paradigm change and an easy-to-use process you can employ to customize your way to happiness. We call this process the 4 x 4 Happiness Model. We're not here to tell you what to do. Life really is a choose-your-own-adventure experience. But we can show you a proven way using key happiness coordinates to figure out *your* best path to a happier place—your very own happiness map to a more fulfilling life. **If you want real-life results, keep reading.** We'll share stories, ask hard questions, and offer resources you can use to apply the simple framework and process to your own work and life.

For easier reading, we both speak with one shared voice throughout the book. However, there will be some sections where each of us will share a unique story or perspective. Because we have such diverse backgrounds, we thought it would be helpful at times to hear our different viewpoints. When we do, you'll see "Emily's Outlook" or "Anthony's Outlook" to keep you from getting disoriented.

WHO ARE WE AND WHY THIS BOOK?

Before we hit the trail together, you may be wondering what in the world brought Anthony—a former inner-city, African-American businessman who's married with children, and Emily—a Caucasian, middle-class, single and female therapist—together to write a book about happiness. Our backgrounds, and even parts of our current realities, are quite different, and that's one of the main reasons why we did this. We wanted to demonstrate that two people of different genders from two very different walks of life and shaped by radically different cultural backgrounds could apply the same framework and process to reach the same destination—*happiness*.

In our research on happiness, we found that people often said happiness was contingent upon something else in life. We call this the *"If Only"* happiness theory. People say, "If only I had a better job, I'd be happy" or "If only I had more money so I could buy that car/house/etc., I would be happy" or "If I were in a romantic relationship or had a better marriage, I'd be happy." The list goes on and on and on. Simply put, by co-authoring this book, we wanted to demonstrate that happiness isn't contingent upon what you have or where you're from. We are here to show you that the "if only" theory falls flat.

ANTHONY'S OUTLOOK

I originated from poverty. A substantial portion of my life was spent in the "hood" with a broken family plagued by abuse, addiction, and poverty among other issues. As an African-American, I came from generations of an oppressed family where the law, and later the system, placed many barriers on escaping poverty's vicious cycle. Yet I was the first in my family to graduate college with a four-year degree and create a pipeline to build generational wealth. I continue to be happily married, which is a statistical anomaly for men from my background. I had a hard life early on and sacrificed mightily to be where I am today. I worked myself out of poverty and now help thousands emerging in the next generation to do the same through our non-profit organization *The Gifted Foundation* (www.iamgifted.org).

I am a committed father and loving husband willing to do the hard work to be present in my kids' lives while pushing forward in my career. I have hard conversations about marriage and work to get through the challenges found in every marriage. Though many family members still live in the same place where I grew up, I have chosen to move forward without forgetting my past. I am who I am today because of my past.

A number of my closest friends come from a fairly stable family lineage with several generations of wealth. They've managed to acquire a quality education. As a result, life has been mostly joyous for them. Me? Not quite the same story. I was born to a teenage mother in Memphis, Tennessee who gave birth to me only thirty-eight days after her 17th birthday and just prior to her senior year at Central High School.

While the purpose of this book is not to give a treatise on generational cycles, I know first-hand how repeated patterns of mostly negative behavior can shape perspectives. They certainly have informed my own "pursuit of happiness."

For example, my mother was abandoned as a small child and relegated to living with her elderly paternal grandparents (my great grandparents). Her mother had a second grade education, suffered five nervous breakdowns, managed to survive the welfare system, and passed away as a victim of cancer at the youthful age of sixty-two. My maternal grandfather, on the other hand, had a respected career as a truck driver but was a severe alcoholic in his early days. He traveled incessantly and was not healthy enough to care for my mother and her two younger siblings.

Much to her credit, my mother fought for her life and mine by doing everything in her power to break the negative generational bonds. Regardless of her efforts, the jaws of poverty, the lack of family support, and not having a post-secondary education—as well as many other detrimental factors—shaped what she could or couldn't offer me as a child. Due to the absence of my biological father and the severe brokenness of my relationship with my stepfather (who did eventually provide some financial stability), I was naturally inclined to let the cultural influences of the world shape me as I grew.

Immediately following my primary education years, which were all spent in economically depressed areas such as South Memphis and Orange Mound, my stepfather got a promotion at Memphis Light, Gas & Water, our local utility company. He and my mother began discussing a move to a different area of the city. Simultaneously, the Hickory Hill community— at one point *the* dream place to live in Memphis for African Americans—was experiencing "white flight" as those who had the resources—mostly whites—were moving farther east of the city. Even then, we couldn't afford to live there, but because my mom was an office secretary at a construction management firm, the CEO who owned a property in that community helped us get it at a substantially reduced cost. So, we moved just prior to my middle school years, and I was bussed to a predominately white, wealthy suburban school, Germantown Middle.

It felt like my world had been turned upside down. I was overwhelmed and felt like an "outsider." I was called every name you could imagine, including the n-word. I got into numerous fights that first year with peers, frequented the principal's office, ran away from home, had constant tension with my mother and stepfather, and even received my first suspension from school. I was a wreck but had no one in my life healthy enough to help me navigate the pain. In fact, the residue of that most difficult year of my life remains with me even as an adult.

Everything changed for me when I scored in the top 1% in the country on a standardized test in 7th grade. I got a letter in the mail right before my 8th grade year stating that I would be placed in a class for high achievers. While this was clearly a fantastic thing to help me turn my life around, there was a downside to this shift in many ways.

I became obsessed with getting approval in the face of what I interpreted as racism, pursuing achievement, and accumulating stuff (material possessions). Little did I know how these obsessions would negatively impact my life and take me down an even darker, more painful path. I spent the remainder of middle school, all of high school, all of college, and the early years of my career searching for love, validation, and approval. I thought if I could get the approval of my peers, achieve more than everyone else, and exhibit success by acquiring more stuff, then I would be able to satiate the pain on the inside. I would be happy.

That didn't work. In fact, it was disastrous. The more I fought to escape the pain I was feeling on the inside, the more I was buried by the very things I was trying to escape. I was looking for love, peace, and happiness in all the wrong places.

Does that sound familiar to you? If you haven't experienced something similar, maybe you know someone else who has faced similar challenges. Maybe you continue to look for love, peace, and happiness in all the wrong places. If so, this book is for you. Emily and I want to provide a newfound perspective on defining happiness using our 4 x 4 Happiness Model. Believe me, it's been proven in the school of hard knocks (I've got the bruises and scars to prove it). Our goal is to empower you to move beyond the greatest pain in your life to live the fulfilling life you've always desired and deserved to live.

EMILY'S OUTLOOK

My life couldn't have been more different than Anthony's if we had scripted it to be so. I grew up in the primarily Caucasian suburbs of Northeast Atlanta with married, biological parents and a sister. My parents were college and masters-educated, and their parents were college-educated, as well, so my generational cycles were quite different than Anthony's. In my family and extended family, lifelong marriages were the norm as were Sunday church attendance, fiscal responsibility, and successful careers. Vacations to Disney World, summer camps, and private school were all part of my version of *normal*.

Ever since I can remember, people would call us the "perfect family" and the sound of those two words was like nails on a chalkboard every time. My dad was a small business owner, and my mom was my vice principal at school, ran political campaigns, and led in our community. We were the kids who had perfect attendance in Sunday school, always participated in youth group, extracurricular sports, and honors classes. Yet underneath all this nauseating perfection was a lot of pain. I experienced childhood trauma, PTSD, anxiety disorders, and medical issues. These were things they didn't talk about in Saturday morning cartoons and certainly not in Sunday school sharing circles.

It wasn't just one trauma or one type of trauma, so with each new trauma or challenge, starting at age five, I was left even more confused, scared, and alone. I didn't know how to process what had happened. I didn't know that I could be angry or sad or just *be*. I also knew that people in our community looked up to my family, so I had to keep it together and play the part. So I just shoved it all deep down inside, slapped on a cliché Bible verse, and forced a smile like a good girl.

When kids experience trauma, they often develop some sort of neurosis to deal with the trauma, to hold the pain. For me, I was riddled with fear and anxiety that later developed into OCD, social anxiety, general anxiety disorder, eating disorders, and several bouts of depression, much of which was undiagnosed until my early twenties. It was normal to me, like when you don't know how poor your vision is until you go to the eye doctor and they show you lenses that allow you to actually read all of those little letters on the board. I thought fear was normal, and life was simply more painful for some than others. When other students would joke about wanting my perfect life, I knew I wouldn't wish it upon even my greatest enemy. Oh, the secrets we keep!

Anxiety is one of the few mental health disorders that can look good on the surface so I didn't have to deal with it, nor did I want to. I channeled it in ways that got me praised and recognized. I became a star student to overcompensate for my low self-esteem and confidence. I'd have stomachaches over the smallest assignments and study far beyond the point of necessity just to ensure I got the best grade possible. Teachers commended me, but I never felt like I could do or be enough. I remember beating myself up to the point of tears in 8th grade for getting a high A on a test simply because it wasn't a perfect score. "I'm worthy if" and "I'm lovable when" were all statements attached to achievement or other's approval of me. These statements became the core beliefs that created a false assumption about happiness. Eventually, I decided I was sick and tired of being sick and tired. I realized there were some things I couldn't change, no matter the level of commitment, desire, or work. My situation didn't change, but my perspective did. At some point early in my own counseling journey, I decided I would fight for healing in my own life so I could help others do the same. Fast forward to today. I'm running a private therapy practice working with "high functioning" high school and college students struggling with anxiety. Now I help students, many of who grew up like me and go to private schools like the ones I attended. They are ivy-league-bound, as were their parents and their parents' parents. Working with these students means I spend about a third of my time consulting and coaching with parents. Many parents make it clear they will pay or do whatever it takes to help their child. Some even try to hire me to live at their home or fly in their private jet to help their college student in crisis. I know the pressure to look perfect and be perfect. It helps me connect to these students even more. My story is not their story, of course, but I understand that the happy images they or their families promote on social media and in their annual Christmas cards might not be 100% accurate.

While Anthony's background and current client base is on one end of the socioeconomic spectrum through his work with the Gifted Foundation, I, and the families I love to work with are on the far opposite end. I'm female and he's male. He's African-American and married. I'm Caucasian and single. He's a dad of two sweet kids, and I can't even take care of a plant to save my life! His parents were never married, and mine are still married. He grew up in a lower-class neighborhood while I grew up in a mid-to-upper-class setting. In other words, we've been on both sides of many fences in life and can tell you that the grass is *not* greener on either side. It's easy to disqualify someone when he or she has what you want or don't want, but collectively, we can assure you that happiness isn't found in a career, family, financial status, etc. Not everyone will completely relate to Anthony or me, but I'm pretty sure you can find yourself somewhere in some parts of our story. That's why we are writing this together. Our goal is to show that, no matter what side of the fence you find yourself on right now, happiness is attainable for you.

Your 4 Happiness Coordinates: We propose 4 key life coordinates based on our own experiences, informed by our personal and professional observations, and supported by the latest research. If you get it right in these 4 areas—Family, Financial, Community, and Physical—you significantly increase the likelihood of experiencing happiness on your life journey. But the four coordinates help you find your bearings *only* when your life GPS is enabled by another universal force—Purpose.

Interestingly, although it was not our design, the most recent Gallup-Sharecare Well-Being Index also found similar key indicators of happiness. First and foremost was Purpose. We agree. It is foundational. Their remaining top four indicators also aligned with our four key life coordinates, although our definitions of them differ: Social, Financial, Community, and Physical. In other words, we're not the only ones seeing this pattern play out in life experiences.

Your 4 Fulfillment Factors: we suggest applying four factors to each of the above coordinates to get clarity for your journey. We'll challenge you to apply them after we consider each coordinate:

1. **Destination**—Where do I want to go in this area (and why)?

2. **Location**—Where am I now?

3. **Realization**—What do I need to change to close the gap?

4. **Acceleration**—How can I best move forward consistently?

THE JOURNEY AHEAD

We've so enjoyed handcrafting this book especially for you and hope you're ready for an exciting journey to discover how to apply the 4 x 4 Happiness Model. Remember, this book will not make you happy, but it can show you how to

get there and equip you for the journey. We refuse to give you just another theory about happiness to talk about at parties. Information without application becomes stagnation. We'll walk you through the personalized, handcrafted, way for YOU to become happier in your own life. It's not a one-size-fits-all model, so we aren't going to tell you one specific way to achieve this goal because that just won't work. No way around it; you'll need to go deep.

Sure, we could have called this book *5 Simple Steps to Happiness* and, no doubt, sold a lot of copies, but long-term change requires unpacking the underlying motives. Our 4 x 4 Happiness Model may be simple, but applying it won't be easy. (That's why so many people aren't happy.)

If you embrace the paradigm and the process we'll unpack on our journey together, we're confident you *will* become happier. To help you prepare for the journey, we invite you to take our quiz to discover *How Happy Are You?* We encourage you to take the simple assessment now and again at the end of the book to compare your results with your second to have for comparison. But for now, take the assessment and ponder what the results might say about your happiness levels right now. Visit TheHappinessMapBook.com now to take the simple assessment.

We want you to be happy, but only *you* can do what must be done to reach that destination. Being stuck in the rat race, over-extending our budgets and ourselves, popping pills to fake a smile, and treading water to live up to the Joneses isn't thriving; it's barely surviving! If you are sick and tired of being sick and tired, it might be time to reroute your life GPS. Are you ready? Let's do this!

Welcome to The Happiness Map.

A NOTE FROM ANTHONY AND EMILY

As a therapist, Emily hears the same question throughout the day being asked between tears and frustrated sighs of hard-working high school students, stay at home parents, and busy executives: *When will I be happy?* And it's not just them; it's all of us asking this question. This is why we wrote the book—for them and for you. And in order to get a substantial answer, one that makes buying this book and spending your precious time reading it, you'll need to engage in the process as well. The questions at the end of each chapter encourage you to interact with what you just read, requiring you to explore, probe and process your own past story, present reality, and future goals. Give yourself permission to ponder these questions for more than a moment and allow yourself the time to consider how you've been conditioned to think about fulfillment in work, relationships, finances, and life in general. We also believe that information without application often leads to stagnation and further frustration, so some of the questions will not only encourage further thought but also action steps to achieve happiness now. We've been intentional about giving you space to write and encourage you to use it. So, grab a good cup of coffee or tea, find a few quiet moments each day in the midst of the

common stressors of life. Silence your phone (it will be ok;
we promise).

BOTTOM LINE

- This book won't automatically make you happy, but it can show you how to get there and equip you for the journey.

- Happiness isn't contingent upon what you have or where you're from.

- Living according to an "if only" outlook will always fall flat.

- Information without application becomes stagnation and leads to additional frustration.

- You can achieve happiness, but only *you* can do what must be done to reach that destination.

HAPPINESS NOW QUESTIONS

1. What do you want out of this book?

_____

_____

2. How was "happiness" defined for you as a child?

_____

_____

3. How do you define "happiness" now?

_____

_____

4. Are you happy? If not, when was the last time you were?

_____

_____

5. Do you believe you *can* be happy?

_____

_____

6. Where has your search for happiness taken you in the past? What have you found helpful and what has left you unsatisfied?

_____

_____

7. On a scale of 1 to 10 (10 being the most significant) how much do the circumstances and people around you influence your happiness?

_____

_____

8. What is currently the single greatest barrier to happiness in your life?

_____

_____

WHAT REALLY
MAKES US HAPPY

"Here is what the scientific research is finding about happiness: we are wired to experience happiness, but we keep hitting the wrong buttons in our efforts to turn our happiness on."

—Henry Cloud

. . . .

BIG IDEA
What really matters to you?

. . . .

We all want to be happy, don't we? We all desire to wake up every morning and look forward to the day ahead. Each of us would love to have a fulfilling life—a life where we're thriving in every aspect of our being. Yet, why is it that so many people seem to live a life so different from what they say they want? People say they want a life of joy, peace, and prosperity, yet many are living a life saturated with pain, sorrow, and disappointment.

Why? We suggest that for many, if not most, we've been misled about what really makes us happy. We let culture define happiness for us. Culture tells us:

How beauty is defined. If you don't fit culture's definition of beauty, you must not be beautiful.

Where and how to live. If your house isn't the largest in the wealthiest community your city has to offer, you couldn't possibly experience joy.

What to drive and what that says about your success. If you don't drive the most expensive, newest, and fastest vehicle with the most bells and whistles, you're incapable of arriving at happiness.

How to build our careers. If you don't get a "good-paying" job, climb the corporate ladder, and work until you retire at a country club and play golf the rest of your life, you must not have lived a fulfilling life.

While these are just a few thoughts, the list could go on and on. But you get the point. An immense amount of pressure from the world around us wants to define our happiness by what everyone else says it should be. This constant pressure means we must weed out distractions in our lives and not allow negative peer and cultural pressures to strangle the authenticity (and joy) out of us. No two human beings are, quite literally, exactly the same. Even identical twins have different passions, desires, ambitions, likes, dislikes, and emotional structures.

If we're all wired so differently, why do we spend so much time trying to be like everyone else and thinking *that* will make us happy. Ever think about that? We know. It's deep. Go ahead and sit there for a second. More importantly, why do we think that if we don't live our lives *better* than everyone else, we've failed? We suggest that the reason so many of us aren't happy is that we're pursuing happiness as defined by someone else. No wonder it's not working. We are not they! And it probably isn't working for them either because they are most likely comparing their happiness to someone else, too!

MAYBE IT'S TIME WE REIMAGINED
HAPPINESS AS SOMETHING SIMPLER
AND LESS COMPLICATED.

We came across two definitions of the word *happy* that could be helpful to compare. The first and probably more common definition comes from Merriam-Webster's Dictionary. Here, happiness is defined as, "feeling pleasure and enjoyment because of your life, situation, etc."[2]

While we might naturally be drawn to the words *pleasure* or *enjoyment* in that definition, we suggest there is a more critical word—*because*. *Because* is easily overlooked because it is a conjunction. By definition, a conjunction identifies a critical connection. In this case, it is an *if this, then that* connection. To make the connection clearer, let's reword the definition thus: "*If* I feel pleasure or enjoyment in my life, *then* my current situation must be a good one." Most people live in the *if this, then that* space when it comes to happiness. They gauge how happy they are primarily by the circumstances around them. "Because" is more than just a conjunction; it's a subordinating conjunction. It connects two parts of the sentence and the subordinating part explains the other part of the sentence. Your life, situation, etc. may be the subordinated part. So, *because* is explaining how we get those feelings of pleasure and enjoyment. But does this really lead to true happiness?

In truth, we have little to no control over most circumstances in life. Yet we often let circumstances dictate our feelings. Consequently, if we live by this first definition, happiness becomes all about where we happen to be at any moment in life or what has happened to us lately. *Did I get the promotion or not? Did I get the car I wanted or not? Did I experience a great vacation or not? Did life unfold the way I wanted it to or not?* Life becomes all about what we *feel* relative to momentary outcomes. When we feel great, it's because something, someone, or some event has gone our way or recently influenced us to feel great.

Don't misunderstand; it's fantastic when good things happen. And its normal to celebrate those good things, as long as you remember that those same things could also become an excuse to be depressed if they don't work out the way you want.

That new-car smell only lasts so long. The vast majority of people do not marry their first love. People can—and will—disappoint you. Welcome to life! When those negative outcomes happen and things don't turn out the way you had hoped, it's easy to feel indifferent, down and out, hopeless, or full of despair *if* your happiness is tied to what happens to you.

But allowing your happiness to be governed by what you feel in the moment can be a dangerous way to live. Your emotional filter isn't always clean. It will get clogged by the pain of ambiguity, displeasure, hurtful moments, and even hurtful people. For many, life becomes so painful that their emotional filter not only clogs, it gets obliterated. Regardless of your background, socioeconomic status, race, gender, or even sexual orientation, at some point in life, you *will* experience pain. It's inevitable.

So, if you base your fulfillment in work and life on whatever is happening to you in the moment, you'll never maintain any level of fulfillment—at least not one that's sustainable. As sensations change, life throws curve balls, friends walk out, family members turn away, or the economy shifts, your happiness will ping pong all over the place. If you base your hopes for a fulfilling life on everything going your way, you're in for a rough ride. No doubt, you've heard the cliché, "Life's full of ups and downs." Most people would prefer to hit the pause button after "ups" and enjoy only the sunny side of life.

> THE PRIMARY CAUSE
> OF UNHAPPINESS IS NEVER
> THE SITUATION BUT YOUR
> THOUGHTS ABOUT IT.
>
> E. TOLLE

But if you never have any *downs*, how will you ever truly understand and appreciate the value of the *ups*? You can and should enjoy the *ups*, while also equipping yourself with the internal tools needed to navigate the *downs*. Life won't always be easy, and it almost never turns out exactly as you plan. But you control how you respond to what happens. You have a choice. And with that choice comes great power.

Happiness is an inside job. We discovered a second, fuller definition of *happy* when we dug a bit deeper: "enjoying or characterized by well-being or contentment."[3] Contentment means, "pleased or satisfied; not needing more." But who decides what you need? *You do.* No person or external circumstance decides whether you are content, happy, or fulfilled. You have the power to choose. Believe it or not, you can choose contentment and fulfillment, even in the face of adversity.

Now, let's be candid: this internal path to happiness is far more difficult than letting outside factors control it. Why? You must discipline yourself every day not to allow your circumstances to govern your emotions and dictate your level of fulfillment. That takes a lot of work. What doesn't take a lot of work is grabbing a bowl of popcorn, plopping on the couch, kicking your feet up, pointing the remote, watching media and propaganda, and allowing your personal narrative to be shaped by whatever comes through the screen.

That's why most people let outside forces shape their narrative. We don't want to sit with ourselves and see what isn't working. We don't want to question our unrealistic expectations about outside circumstances fixing what we haven't been addressing on the inside. We allow our internal perspectives, and thus our fulfillment in work and life, to be shaped by what we hear the most. As natural as that may be, when we allow this path of least resistance to guide us, our belief systems, values, lifestyle choices, work ethic, career choices, relationships, and more can all be traced back to what we see on television or what we absorb through unhealthy propaganda and through negative circles of friends doing the same thing. Garbage in. Garbage out.

As you think about how you have defined happiness to this point in life, we hope you're willing to stick with us as we reimagine it together in the pages to come. Even if the first definition of happiness based on pleasure and enjoyment resonates more with where you are today, we invite you to fight for something more—*fulfillment*.

Fight for fulfillment in work and life! You don't have to wait for happiness to find you. You already have the power and authority to make your work and life truly extraordinary!

ANTHONY'S OUTLOOK

Have you ever paused to ask yourself, *what does "better" mean to me?* If you're like most people, the odds are you have not taken the time to define your version of *better*. As a result, you are probably not as happy as you want to be because you're distracted by what the world around you says you must be to be happy, which seems to me to be a painful way to live.

I've been there before and, trust me, I was miserable. It's the primary reason why, at the age of twenty-four, I chose to walk away from corporate America and pursue what I actually loved to do—impact people first and not focus solely on material wealth. Just about everybody in my family and friendship circle thought I was nuts to walk away from the promise of long-term corporate promotion.

I was blessed to graduate as *Top Student* in my major from The University of Memphis, the top sales degree program in the country at that time. I had job offers from Coca-Cola, Kraft Foods, Philip Morris, RJ Reynolds, Saks Incorporated, Cummins Engines, and many more Fortune 500 companies. An incredible professor encouraged me to work for RJ Reynolds Tobacco because his wife worked for the company and experienced tremendous success during her tenure. I took the gig in spite of the fact that it did not align with my core values (I don't smoke or drink). In hindsight, I took it because I was promised the world financially. Had I stayed, I am convinced I would have earned millions of dollars on that path.

Fortunately for me, and many others around me, I realized I was chasing money and career success, thinking it would make me happy. It only makes sense that a kid who rose above the ranks of poverty to be the first in his family to graduate from college would choose the most lucrative career path, right? It made sense to my mom and stepfather; it made sense to my peers; it made sense to my professors. It even made sense to me on the surface, as I had been conditioned throughout my entire life to color inside the lines and stay within the confines of "the system."

In hindsight, it was a terrible, shortsighted decision based on what others thought would work for me. I soon discovered I was doing what made others happy while I was miserable. I had the company car, expense account, generous salary, a bonus structure, and the promise to be placed on the fast track. Yet, I didn't like what I saw in the mirror every morning. I wasn't happy. My sales territory of Tupelo, MS was number one in the entire U.S. We were selling more cigarettes than anyone else in the nation. I was at the top and poised to go higher. The problem was that I defined "at the top" differently than most.

I took the call from a search firm and eventually transitioned from RJ Reynolds to 3M (another Fortune 100 giant) as a Cardiopulmonary Specialist. I realized at our first national meeting that I was the youngest person in the country in my role and the only African-American male. I remember one associate asking me, "Anthony, how did you manage to pull this off?" To be candid, being in that position felt great for bragging purposes. Once again, however, there was a never-ending battle within me. I hated the unfulfilled person I saw everyday in the mirror.

My personal joy is ultimately driven by the lives I impact, not by how much money I make. I didn't know that at the time, but I eventually evolved to reach that conclusion. After only a year at 3M, I walked away. Once again, everyone around me thought I was nuts. My mother and stepfather told me it was the craziest thing I had ever done. Regardless of how they and everyone else felt, I knew I had to define happiness for myself.

I made a choice then to define happiness for myself and to do what I thought God had created me to do. I walked away from it all, took a huge pay cut, and certainly limited my long-term potential financial earnings. And I never felt more at peace in my entire life. Since then, I've spoken to so many others who say they wish they had the courage to do the exact same thing, yet it feels impossible to walk away from a steady paycheck and reduce their lifestyles to follow their dreams. In my humble opinion, they're letting culture define happiness for them.

My path is certainly not for the faint-of-heart. I'm not crazy enough to believe otherwise. And my life isn't easy now. If you're anything like me, you have to get up everyday and grind so you can keep the machine running. I get that and completely understand. Yet, you can still maximize value in life and live with a peace that surpasses human understanding. But you have to be willing to exercise the mental discipline required to do so. It's worth it—the battle to keep real happiness at the forefront whatever it takes! Let's find your way to a more fulfilling place in work and life.

EMILY'S OUTLOOK

My mom was also my English teacher in our private school. A lover of literature, she helped our entire class of awkward, angsty teenagers enter fascinating and colorful worlds through pages of exceptional literature. She would encourage us to close our eyes as classic pieces were read aloud. At first, a few classmates chuckled, thinking her request was nothing short of ridiculous. After a second of her "don't mess with me" stare, they quickly closed their eyes as well. She read with careful voice inflexion and tonal changes. When a sentence had particular importance, she'd allow for a long but pensive pause. She was no longer reading simple prose, she was bringing the words to life, and we were transported from our simple classroom to exhilarating places.

I remember hearing Shakespearean sonnets that spoke so deeply to my soul and made me want to experience love the way his characters possessed it. I remember William Blake or Edgar Allan Poe and wondering what painful situations in their past gave them the material to write such sometimes dreadful and grim poems. But I had a special connection with one poem in particular by Jenny Joseph entitled "When I Am An Old Woman I Shall Wear Purple." It's about a woman who has lived her entire life living up to everyone's expectations, following the rules, and being meek. She claims that when she's older, she will wear purple and do whatever she wants. She'll eat whatever she wants, break cultural norms, and be impulsive—simply because she can. Towards the end of the poem, she says she just might start some of those behaviors now, thus empowering the reader to do the same. Or at least, that was how I interpreted it:

> But maybe I ought to practice a little now?
> So people who know me are not too shocked
> and surprised when suddenly I am old, and
> start to wear purple.[4]

Forced as a child to attend cotillion classes with white gloves and manners lessons, I loved the idea of throwing social niceties to the wind. And ever since dieting started in my mid teens, the idea of eating whatever I wanted sounded heavenly! To me, growing up and growing old meant freedom from societal pressures because, like the poem stated, *at some point in life we will just stop caring.* In my youth, I didn't have perspective, so I coveted the freedom. Unbeknownst to me, my instincts were accurate—and now we have the research to prove it!

Researchers have identified one of the common denominators of a happy, satisfied life is age. In our youth-obsessed world, one would think that wrinkle-free youth should be the happiest of all. They look and feel their best; they have their whole lives in front of them filled with untapped potential. But the age-to-happiness connection is a bit more complex. Countless studies portray a U-shaped paradigm to depict the relationship between age and happiness.

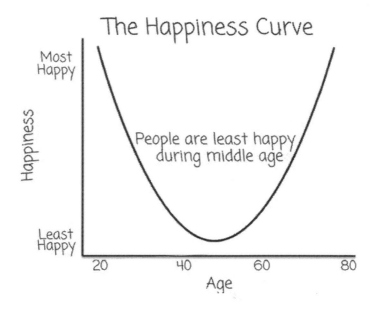

Happiness is high in youth, decreases significantly in the late 40s, then increases from age 50 onward. To be more specific, the National Bureau of Economic Research says Americans are least happy between the ages of 45 and 49.[5] Why? What things and which people influence our happiness will naturally differ at various ages.

In our 20s...

- Being young & physically fit
- More freedom
- Getting married
- Having children
- Limited expenses
- Wide social network
- Freedom with schedule & social life

In our 30s...

- Having children
- Feeling confident and more self-assured
- Getting married
- Making more money and progressing in career
- Buying a home

In our 40s...

- Feeling more comfortable with self
- Good family life
- Enjoying kids as they grow up
- Career advancement
- More savings

In our 50s...

- More emotionally grounded
- Paying off mortgage
- Traveling
- Children moving out
- Becoming a grandparent
- Looking towards retirement in future years

60s and Beyond

- Retirement
- Enjoy more hobbies & interests
- Ability to relax & appreciate life
- Time to focus on self

Where do you find yourself on this age and happiness dynamic? It's important to consider your current season of life as you assess what really makes you happy. As you think about your current life stage, do you agree with these findings? If anything is missing, feel free to add your personal thoughts in the additional space offered in each age bracket.

HOW HAPPY ARE YOU?

What do you say about happiness? How do you define it? And just how happy are you *really?* To further define happiness, S. Oishi and E.A. Gilbert say, "A happy person is characterized as someone who 'has pleasant feelings most of the time, and feels satisfied with his/her life overall.'" So, how satisfied are you with life overall? Have you ever paused long enough to think about what truly matters to you and whether or not you are sincerely happy? Are you living someone else's dreams or your own? Are you living vicariously through your spouse, children, closest friends, a reality television show, a celebrity, or some other source that gives you a false sense of the joy you long to have permanently in your life? Are you trying to achieve fulfillment at work based on someone else's definition of what it means to be fully engaged?

We encounter people all the time who wish they were doing something different with their lives. They're living out someone else's agenda, unsatisfied with their current position in work and life, yet they don't have the courage to do what it takes to walk a different path. They keep doing the same things in the office and wonder why they aren't feeling more fulfilled at work. They continue the same self-defeating life habits and don't understand why their life doesn't feel more fulfilling. The hamster wheel of life keeps accelerating, convincing them that the wheel is moving far too swiftly for them to actually escape. So, instead of pursuing the discipline required to make the necessary alterations, they concede to the pain and allow the day-to-day routine to defeat them. Life becomes a grind, far from the happiness they hoped to have by now. It doesn't have to be this way.

ANTHONY'S OUTLOOK

When my wife was a college student, she babysat for one of the most successful families in the city of Memphis. The husband was a prominent doctor, arguably the most recognized specialist in his field. During the last dialogue we had with him many years ago, he said if he could walk away from it all and simply write novels, he would do it in a heartbeat. Almost two decades later, guess what he is doing? Still practicing medicine. Why? He hasn't exercised the courage required to do what he ultimately enjoys full-time.

Unfortunately, this is the case for many people, perhaps even you. Emily and I are not saying you need to leave your job—not at all. In fact, the best way forward for you may be thinking differently about your role right where you are. Not everyone has the luxury of doing what they love and earning a living simultaneously. But the list of things holding you back from doing that is smaller than you'd think. Whether or not you actually have the skills to produce in your area of passion will go a long way in determining the possibilities. For example, if I woke up tomorrow morning and decided to follow a passion for singing, my wife would likely pack her belongings, take the kids, and head for higher ground because my family would drown in a hurry. When God was handing out gifts, I was not in the line for anything related to musical talent. I would *truly* be nuts to compete with the most angelic voices, artists, and musicians in the world. However, when God was handing out gifts for inspiring others, moving people to act on their hearts' desires, and supporting them with developing practical game plans for seeing their dreams come to life, I believe I made the cut.

I could have continued selling cigarettes with RJ Reynolds or pharmaceutical products with 3M and both would have provided a decent financial living for my family. But, I wouldn't be happy and that would have dramatically affected my work, and eventually my family as well. My wife and children would feel the repercussions of my dissatisfaction if I were not operating in my sweet spot.

Because of my decision to pursue what matters most to me, I have been blessed to impact tens of thousands of lives. And I am just getting started. Who knows? Those numbers could reach into the millions eventually. It pains me to think of what might have happened had I continued to sell cigarettes for a living. It ought to pain you to think of getting up one more day knowing you are miserable with where you are in life.

You should want more for yourself than punching the proverbial clock for one more day. Let's be clear: We're not trying to inspire you to make a senseless decision to pursue your passions at the expense of priorities and responsibilities. We're not encouraging you to do anything crazy like quit your job, leave your spouse, walk out on your children, or anything else resembling an isolated, unplanned decision.

> WHAT WE ARE SUGGESTING IS THAT YOU BEGIN TO MENTALLY PREPARE TO LIFT YOURSELF OUT OF WHATEVER RUT YOU FIND YOURSELF IN NOW.

You can start taking the small, practical steps toward the happier place for which you long. As Joe Sabah said, "You don't have to be great to start, but you do have to start to be great."

Is it risky? Yes. Difficult? Sure. But if you stay where you are, life is going to be hard, too, with no possibility of living a deeply-fulfilling life. You get to choose your hard. Entrepreneur, author, and motivational speaker Jim Rohn, makes the choice clear: "We must all suffer from one of two pains: the pain of discipline or the pain of regret. The difference is discipline weighs ounces while regret weighs tons."

Take the time to sit down, script out what you honestly desire to see in your life today, and be willing to make the necessary adjustments to begin pursuing that reality. If you don't do it, you can be sure no one else will do it for you.

Are you in?

THE BOTTOM LINE

- When we let culture define happiness for us, it's never fully satisfying.
- Many of us aren't happy because we're comparing our happiness with others and pursuing happiness defined by someone else.
- Momentary happiness never leads to sustainable levels of fulfillment.
- Happiness is a choice. It's an inside job.
- Life isn't easy, and it almost never turns out exactly as you plan. But you control how you respond to what happens.
- Getting to your happiness destination requires decision and precision. We never stumble upon our dreams and happiness.

HAPPINESS NOW QUESTIONS

1. In your search for happiness, to whom do you tend to compare your life?

   _____

   _____

2. How might you have let others' definitions of happiness shape your own thoughts about how you see happiness in work and life?

   _____

   _____

3. Where do you look to define happiness? Social media, family, friends, colleagues?

   _____

   _____

4. It's important to consider your current season of life as you assess what really makes you happy. Where do you find yourself on the U-shaped age and happiness dynamic?

_____

_____

5. Are you satisfied with where you are in this stage of life? Why or why not?

_____

_____

6. What advice would you offer to the younger version of yourself in search for happiness?

_____

_____

7. What advice do you think the 80-year-old version of yourself would tell you now in your search for happiness?

_____

_____

8. Consider taking a 24-48 hour "fast" from things that leave you feeling less than satisfied with your life. Fill the time with life-giving activities like those listed below.

_____

_____

A NAVIGATION TOOL

People recharge in different ways depending on whether you are an introvert or extrovert. Contrary to popular belief, introverts can be quite social and extroverts can be the quieter people in a crowd. If you recharge best with people, pull ideas from the extrovert list. If you recharge best by being alone or with a few people, look at the introvert list:

Extrovert:

- Invite your neighbors or a new person at work over for dinner and buy a fun game to keep the conversation going.
- Serve in a local outreach or ministry and use your skillset to meet a need in your community. Get to know those with whom you are serving.
- Join a group fitness class or outdoors club to meet others who are interested in similar activities. Push yourself physically and have fun doing it!

Introvert:

- Take five to ten minutes at the beginning and end of the day to write down positive things, interactions, and outcomes daily. This powerful practice will help you focus more on the positive than the negative each day.
- Spend time in mindfulness or "breath prayers," either on your own or at a place of worship.
- Invite one or two close friends to your house, and catch up over an unrushed meal. Create a theme for each evening by discussing topics you/your guest find interesting.

FIND YOUR DOT
AND OWN IT!

*"Direction—not intention—
determines our destination."*

—Andy Stanley

. . . .

BIG IDEA
Do you know where you are on the
journey to happiness?

. . . .

Y ou are here. In a chaotic world, those can be comforting words. Whenever we get lost, we quickly scan a map to find the clarifying dot that indicates our location. Whether it's the gigantic map in the middle of a crowded mall or a navigation phone app used to get through hectic rush hour traffic in the city, knowing where we are is critical if we ever hope to reach our desired destinations. So it is in life as we search for happiness. Once you know where you want to go, you must then figure out where you are. Find your dot and own it.

As a culture, we're often obsessed with the *next* best thing to distract us from reflecting on our current realities. Reflecting on our current reality can be messy and uncomfortable. For some it feels like doing nothing. For others, it lacks the satisfaction that comes from being busy. And like cleaning a messy closet, the beginning of self-examination can feel overwhelming. Then we start losing momentum and engage in escape tactics like binge-watching TV shows, surfing the web, or shopping. At least the mess is confined to the closet, as long as we don't open the door. But in work and life, if we truly want happiness, we can't avoid the painful consequences of avoidance forever, even if we have to get messy for a bit.

EMILY'S OUTLOOK

In my own childhood, I remember "forced family time" spent cleaning neglected areas like the notorious "stuff drawer" in the kitchen, outdated fridge food, or the hall closet that held tons of random items, including clothes I thought were long lost. The shock we had when finding those items was the only silver lining on those long cleaning days. Taking everything out and spreading it all across the counter or floor made the initial cleaning process look like more of a mess than anything else.

We'd put the radio in the hallway so everyone could hear oldie songs by *The Temptations* and *The Jackson 5* to make the time more bearable. The beginning was the worst, but after hours of sorting, purging, and organizing, we proudly displayed the organized spaces that would cause anyone working at the Container Store to swoon. Just like those spring cleaning days, the first part of sorting through your work and life issues is the hardest. But I encourage you to simply open up that metaphorical closet, turn up the music, and let's start unpacking together.

WHERE TO START

Not all of life is good. Sometimes bad things happen to us. Ignoring it won't change anything. Thus, in the process of sifting through our *stuff,* we face the challenging work of acceptance. Acceptance doesn't necessarily mean that we embrace the past pain and current challenges, but it does mean we acknowledge that it happened. Hardships don't have to define us, but we do need to recognize that they have shaped us.

Part of the Law of the Conservation of Mass states that *matter can neither be created nor destroyed; but it can, transform from one form to another.* Just like matter, we can't make the past cease to exist. But if we are intentional, we can transform it into something we can use for good on our journey. We can't make our painful memories, emotions, and experiences disappear.

WE CAN DENY THEM, HIDE THEM, AND PRETEND THEY DIDN'T HAPPEN, BUT THE ONLY WAY TO TRULY MOVE FORWARD IS TO OWN THEM AND GO THROUGH THEM.

When we suppress the past, we become like an emotional volcano, appearing to be calm on the surface but with ferocious activity brewing inside. Someone might say the wrong thing, you might see a picture from years before, or a face on your Facebook feed hits an emotional bruise. In an instant, you realize that the pain never really passed; the grief never left. It was only buried by a constant desire of distraction and denial.

Instead of accepting and growing, some people choose to deny reality through an inward emotional explosion that expresses itself through social isolation, depression, passive-aggressive behaviors, anxiety, and various unhealthy behaviors and disorders. Others choose the outward emotional expression option by letting their emotional volcanoes erupt with rage, misplaced aggression, and certain addictions. Regardless of outward or inward explosions, rejecting reality and the need to process your past and current location will stunt your ability to move forward in your own happiness journey.

EMILY'S OUTLOOK

When I was still in elementary school, my sister, mom, and I were in a horrific car accident. My mom was driving with me in the front seat and my seven-year-old sister in the back. Suddenly, my sister's petite body flew past me into the front dashboard. I hit the front window as glass shattered all over. We had hit a telephone pole and all had concussions. How the two ambulances even reached us was nothing short of a miracle. They transported us to different hospitals. Although my injuries looked more severe initially, my sister's deteriorating state and seizures soon indicated her case was far more acute than originally imagined.

She was quickly rushed into the operating room for emergency surgery for a depressed skull fracture with possible brain damage. After several surgeries and long hospital stays, she was eventually able to rehabilitate and return to normal life months later. At the time, we were only eighteen months apart and really close—matching jumpers, hair bows, and all of it! My sister had coded several times on the operating table and should have been dead. So when she needed help rehabilitating, I was thrilled to serve. She was my hero. As her younger sister, helping her became my new job in life— my identity.

Her story is truly miraculous, and I always loved listening to my parents retell it because it just reminded us all of God's protection and care. But I never really processed all that happened then; I don't think any of us knew how. Looking back, I remember being alone and afraid in the Atlanta Children's Hospital because my mom, dad, and family friends were with my sister in another hospital. I didn't know what was going on and felt terribly scared. While I now know that the accident and the opportunity to care for her was a significant reason I went into the helping profession, I lacked the insight to realize how that experience impacted me.

Our family celebrated God's provision and care, but we didn't process the post-traumatic stress experienced from the trauma. My parents weren't therapists and while they cared greatly for us, I think that they had no idea how powerful childhood trauma can be on children. We were all in survival mode, unaware of the catastrophic impact it would have on all of us, for better or worse. My sister had flashbacks and nightmares for years. She had no idea that she had significant signs of Post-Traumatic Stress Disorder (PTSD). I changed literally overnight. Before the accident, I was an independent, extroverted, free-spirited child. Afterwards, I became a shy, anxious, and hyper-vigilant young girl. As I discovered later in my studies, trauma can have that effect, especially on kids because they are so vulnerable. We all have our specific temperament and personalities that generally stay the same—unless one experiences intense trauma.

After several years of therapy and trauma work, I realized how this event and several others were at the core of my anxiety and struggle with codependency. I needed to hear how God protected me, but I also needed to know that He was close to me in the hospital room when I felt so alone. I came to realize He hadn't abandoned me then, nor would He in the future. I needed to know I didn't have to suppress my fear because God was big enough to handle it.

In the midst of caring for my sister, I formed the belief that asking questions, expressing "negative emotions," or doing anything other than being a silent, good little girl just wasn't acceptable. Now I know, it is not only acceptable, but also a vital part of being human! We all need to know that we are worthy and valuable *because of who we are*, not because of what we do or don't do for others. Yes, it was wonderful that I could serve my sister, but she and others would love me even if I couldn't do anything for them.

I have also learned that bad things are inevitable and none of us are promised good outcomes. Nothing I could *do* would serve as a safeguard from bad things happening in my life no matter how hard I tried. Obedient kids *and* disobedient kids get hurt or abused, neglected, experience abandonment, and witness trauma—not because of what they do, but simply because life can be so broken sometimes. It was critical for me to work through that situation as well as other traumas I experienced in my life in order to be the healthiest and happiest version of myself! If I had not "opened my own closet door," not only would I be a less happy person today, I would also have run the risk of hurting those I try to help because I hadn't been fully healed myself. What I have learned has made me a much more helpful and productive therapist for my own clients.

DON'T IGNORE IT

As author Josephe LaLonde says, "Regardless of how much light or darkness we have in our pasts, we can't allow our pasts to define us.[6] Your future happiness depends on coming to terms with your past and present pain. You might make advances in various areas of life, but if you don't deal with past pain, you rob yourself of priceless growth opportunities and the potential of feeling fulfilled. The call from the doctor, the termination notice from HR, or the divorce papers after twenty-five years of marriage, all serve as reminders that we aren't in control.

Instead of trying to control your realities and minimizing or suppressing the pain, you can choose to process, learn, and grow. Maybe there's a relationship you need to mend, a person needing your forgiveness, or an unhealthy habit you need to address. If a name or situation pops into your head as you read this, don't ignore it. You can buy a new car and achieve some accolade at work, but these past and current painful realities will always hold you back. No matter where you go, you take *you* with you. We encourage you to learn from the past, do the healing work that needs to be done, and weave it into the tapestry of your life as your journey towards living an even better story—like David did.

A CASE STORY

David was a young CEO of a startup in Atlanta. He had worked for years to launch his idea, put his team in place, and partner with key companies utilizing his innovative proprietary products. While the work was rather lucrative and offered recognition among industry leaders, he was deeply depressed. He came to therapy hoping to gain instant insights, so he could quickly change the mood that hindered his work productivity.

For the first session, he came with a notebook and mini-recorder, to catch any of the points he might miss with his note taking. He was motivated. He had mapped out in detail the next twenty years of his life with help from his executive consultant but admitted to having a hard time even getting out of bed in the morning. David's typical day usually consisted of eighteen hours of work, four hours of sleep, one for exercise, and the rest for commuting!

He had maintained that irrational schedule since he started his company years ago. When the manpower behind his company had increased from just him to thirty others, he simply added more onto his plate. He had little time left for a personal life. He was rarely satisfied and often compared his successes with counterparts who had been in the same industry for at least a decade more than he had been.

As the oldest child of a working class, immigrant family, his need to achieve and his unquenchable thirst for success had been strongly reinforced at home. His parents struggled to meet their expenses and worked two to three jobs to pay the bills. They didn't graduate high school and told their kids that the key to success was education, hard work, and always striving to be the best.

David received little daily attention from his overworked and sleep-deprived parents, but they would always recognize his academic accomplishments. David would rarely see his parents, so he cherished the, "I'm proud of you, son," from his father following a perfect report card. His hard work paid off, and he was offered several full-ride scholarships to prestigious ivy-league universities.

His amazing work ethic landed him a highly competitive internship with a top company in Silicon Valley for the summer of his senior year of college. After receiving a job offer at this prestigious firm following graduation, he joined the company for a few years before launching out on his own. As the owner of his company, his lifelong patterns of self-doubt, fear, and over-performance plagued him. He had everything he ever wanted, but he found himself lonely at the top, leaving his office at the late hours of the evening, only to go home to an empty and cold, high-rise condo.

Through therapy, David saw what parts of his life were underdeveloped and often rooted in past pain. Because he wanted his life to be perfect, he had minimized family conflict and unhealthy patterns in his imperfect family relationships. Because he never felt unconditionally loved, he found it difficult to truly love others. He saw how desperately he needed secure attachments and rebirth as a human "being" not a human "doing" in boyhood.

He came to recognize that his deep need for unconditional acceptance was far more satisfying than a paycheck or various industry awards. He worked less, trusted others more, and engaged in activities focused on fun and learning instead of achievement. David allowed himself to own the past pain and use it to inform him about his needs to have greater growth and happiness in his life now.

WHAT ABOUT YOU?

David's situation is similar to many of our own scenarios. We all have certain aspects of our story that are in our control and others that are not. David didn't choose to grow up in an underprivileged home. He didn't choose his birth order. He couldn't fix the inattention from his parents. But as an adult, he recognized his choices and chose to make the most of them.

Like David, do you have any areas from your past that are hindering your growth?

YOU CAN LIVE A FULFILLED LIFE, BUT
YOU CAN'T BEGIN TO MOVE TOWARDS
FULFILLMENT UNTIL YOU KNOW
YOUR CURRENT LOCATION.

We call this "finding your dot." You may have areas in your past that you can own and transform in order to move toward greater happiness. The point is not to wallow in self-pity, but to discover your pain points and understand how they can be used as strengths rather than weaknesses.

Take some time right now to think about the answers to the questions we just asked you. The answers to this question are going to be very important in the next chapter where we reveal how you can choose to be happy even with trauma and pain in your past.

THE BOTTOM LINE

- Your future happiness depends on coming to terms with your past and present pain.
- The only way to grow is "in and through." If you don't deal with your pain, it will come back later and greater.
- What you deny will ultimately drive you. Rejecting reality and the need to process your past and current location will stunt your ability to move forward in your own happiness journey.

HAPPINESS NOW QUESTIONS

1. After reading about Anthony's decision to walk away from success to pursue his dream, what unmet desires do you think of in your own life? Take the time to sit down and write out what you honestly desire to see in your life and your future. Be sure to make the necessary adjustments to begin pursuing that reality.

   • Today:

   _____

   _____

   • Short term (1-5 years):

   _____

   _____

   • Long term (6+ years):

   _____

   _____

2. What parts of your story have you been avoiding?
    (We encourage you to sit with this question for a few
    moments. You might want to include trusted friends, a
    professional, and definitely some time in this process.)
    You don't have to know the plan today. Just take some
    time to consider parts that have been omitted or not
    given the time to process through.

3. On a scale of 1 to 10 (10 being *very* self-aware), where do
    you fall in terms of self-awareness and recognizing your
    position on life and happiness? _____

4. What about David's story resonated with you? What
    similarities are there in your life and David's life?

    _____

    _____

    _____

HAPPINESS IS A CHOICE!

"God, grant me the serenity to accept the things I cannot change, the courage to change the things I can, and the wisdom to know the difference."

—*Reinhold Niebuhr*

· ·

BIG IDEA
Can you *really* choose
to be happy?

· ·

To be happy, you must do happy. What does *that* mean? Instead of making happiness a single, ultimate destination you pursue, choose to embrace the happiness journey as an active and ongoing process—as something you do, not something you desire. Getting the right mindset about happiness ensures that better actions will follow in a cyclical process, making your actions a self-fulfilling prophecy.

When we are happy, we do things that make us more successful. Our feelings direct our actions and our actions impact our feelings. We might call it the circle of happiness. It's a simple, cyclical process we see all the time in psychology and business. When you feel good about yourself, you eat well and exercise, maintain or lose weight, and thus continue to feel good about your appearance. Positive attitudes lead to positive actions, which reinforce the positive attitudes. On the other hand, if you have a crazy workweek without any workouts, you're more likely to order pizza and sit around the house on Saturday with your best friends Ben and Jerry. The same is true in other areas of life such as your work and relationships. When you feel good, you continue to engage in healthy activities and life patterns.

In *The Power of Full Engagement*, Jim Loehr and Tony Schwartz found the wealthiest people are also the most proactive at cultivating healthy behaviors that, in turn, foster greater levels of happiness.[7] These healthy patterns include having positive relationships, maintaining physical health, being mindful, and engaging in other life-giving activities. To illustrate the point, psychologist and professor, Dr. Sonja Lyubomirsky, created a happiness equation:

$$H = S + C + V$$

H (happiness) = S (individual's happiness set point) + C (life circumstances) + V (voluntary or intentional activities)

Lyubomirsky believes our happiness set point (our general level of happiness) is determined by birth or genetics, which account for fifty percent of our happiness, while circumstances such as marital status, salary, and appearances—conditions of living that we often place an inordinate amount of focus on—determine only ten percent.[8] In other words, we have no control over half of it—genetic makeup, our family, the socioeconomic class we were born into, and hereditary diseases or illnesses. Even when faced with devastating circumstances, the low point will be relatively short-lived before we revert back to our normal set point. Jonathan Haidt, author of *The Happiness Hypothesis*[9], found that paraplegics and lottery winners have both, on average, returned to their baseline happiness levels within one year of their life-changing event.

Contrary to popular thought, however, forty percent of happiness comes from voluntary and intentional activities; **things we do to actually change our happiness level.** That's wonderful news! You now know you have the ability to control your happiness by changing life activities and habits. Regardless of the situation, you have the ability to retain your basic outlook on life and do things to increase your happiness.

All too many of us only look at life circumstances as the leading indicator for happiness, yet life circumstances account for only ten percent of the equation. Think about how much time we spend obsessing over that ten percent. No wonder so many people are anxious and depressed! We're focusing primarily on the smallest predictor of happiness and expecting it to change everything. Instead, we need to focus more on what is within our control.

As football coach Tony Dungy says in his book *Quiet Strength*, "You can't always control circumstances. However, you can always control your attitude, approach, and response. Your options are to complain or to look ahead and figure out how to make the situation better."[10] We can only change some things about our lives, but we do have control over how we respond to everything.

PRODUCT VS. PROCESS

Overvaluing the product and undervaluing the growth process is a dangerous byproduct of the American Dream gone wild. We so easily overvalue the landmark moments while minimizing the grunt work that produced the character, strength, and courage needed to achieve those big goals in the first place. The road to character and personal development is just as important as the results, perhaps even more so because we wouldn't have the latter without the former.

Instead of putting our hopes in the American Dream as our only future destination, we need to see the pathway to getting there as even more important. The process of becoming, growing, and learning is critical to whatever success looks like at the end of the journey. The promotion is what we may want at work, but it's the job loss, career changes, and daily challenges that make us who we are and position us to appreciate who we become in the process. The growth process takes time. It's often a byproduct of our own failures. Leaders, inventors, and businesses that paved the way to make our country great routinely attribute their failures as paving the way to their greatest successes.

Arthur Brooks put it this way: "Failure leads to the greatest success, which is humility and learning. In order to fulfill yourself, you have to forget yourself. In order to find yourself, you have to lose yourself."[11] Orville and Wilbur Wright had serious depression and family illnesses as barriers to success. They failed repeatedly before successfully creating an airplane that flew. The same drive they learned from pushing forward in spite of mental health and family issues kept their dream alive when their prototypes didn't fly.

Thomas Edison was told that he was too stupid to learn anything when he was young. He was even fired from a few jobs. He and his team had at least 1,000 unsuccessful attempts when trying to invent a workable electric light bulb until finally achieving success. Edison said, "Our greatest weakness lies in giving up. The most certain way to succeed is always to try just one more time." If he were only motivated by results, he would have given up long before realizing his dream.

More recently, Tyler Perry has grossed more than $845 million after producing, writing, and directing a decade's worth of films and TV shows. But he had a much less glamorous beginning. For several years, his shows flopped, costing him both money and ego. Looking back, however, he said he never failed because each opportunity offered greater learning and growth. "You have to understand that what you may perceive to be a failure may very well be an opportunity to learn, grow, get better, and prepare for the next level. If you find the lessons in what you perceive to be failures, then you won't ever fail at anything." Perry added this key thought: "Everything I learned during the 'learning' years (that's what I call them now) has helped me in the 'harvest' years (that's what I'm living in now). Don't be hard on yourself. You haven't failed. Find the lesson so you can use it when you get to your harvest."[12] And that's the perspective we're talking about that is critical for embracing the Happiness Map process.

What have you learned from failures and challenges over the years? It's easy to push them to the margins of life, to forget the pain of falling short. But remember, the process is just as important as the results. We invite you to step back and think about the moments when you've been able to have influence in someone's life. Perhaps it was a teachable moment with a student, a mentoring situation with an "at-risk" child, or simply parenting your own children. You were probably able to dispense wisdom and share valuable insights *because* you went through your own seasons of growth. When looking back now, it's easy to realize the challenge was worth it, but in the midst of the challenges and trials, each day of growth can feel grueling. Emily knows a thing or two about that.

EMILY'S OUTLOOK

As a child, I had some medical issues requiring treatments and surgeries, one of which was scoliosis of the spine. In the 90s, children with significant curvatures wore body braces 24/7 to hold the curvature of the spine and prevent it from getting worse. The braces were extremely uncomfortable, hot, and so tight it was sometimes hard to breathe. Wearing the brace affected everything because I had to wear certain clothes to accommodate it. I had to leave class early to have it strapped on or taken off so I could participate in some sports—and those were only the physical limitations.

The emotional impact was much worse. I was already an anxious kid due to genetic predisposition, environmental causes, and childhood traumas, but my anxiety only increased by wearing the huge body brace in middle school, a time when everyone desires to just *fit in*. I hated getting attention for it. I hated being different. I went to a school full of cliques, so wearing a brace only highlighted my separation from the "in crowd." Add that to oversized glasses that I had worn since I had Strabismus, also called "crossed eyes", since I was eighteen months old. Even worse, I had a chubby body and hideous bangs I used to cover up my large forehead; *awkward* doesn't even begin to describe middle school for me!

Sometimes I would cry at night because the brace was so painful to wear. But the real pain was inside as I felt tremendously different and uncomfortable with my appearance. I wanted to hide for the 3+ years I needed to wear the brace and come back as a well-adjusted, normal girl. When that wasn't possible, I hid my personality, losing so much of who I was simply because I didn't want to be seen. I used to watch the cliques make fun of the unpopular kids and I realized that being invisible—being unseen—was better than being mocked.

After years of wearing it, my curvature didn't get better. It got worse! I was told that if I did nothing, I'd be bent over ninety degrees before my eighteenth birthday. That was hard news to hear when I was faithfully wearing the brace and not getting the results I wanted. After the doctor visit, I remember breaking down and weeping with my mom. I can still remember where I was in our old house, sitting next to her as I faced yet another unsuccessful brace treatment. In between the sobs, she told me, "Emily, God is cultivating such character in you!"

With tears in my eyes and a heavy heart, I responded, "I'm tired of gaining character; I just want to be normal!" Yes, I valued character, but I just wanted to play with friends, be invited to sleepovers, and sleep without pain. Finally, I had a surgery that corrected the curvature and no longer required me to wear the back brace. The six months to fully recover and my future restrictions from certain sports was nothing compared to those grueling years in the brace.

Looking back, I know now that my experience with scoliosis was pivotal to my becoming a therapist. I gained an appreciation for life and my own health that I carry to this day after so many visits to the orthopedist's office where I saw kids living with prosthetics or bound to wheelchairs. So many doctor and hospital visits gave me a keen awareness of the fellowship of suffering that many parents, children, and families enter when dealing with a negative diagnosis or disease.

I'm not trying to minimize or trivialize the pain by saying our hardships can be of value later in life. However, I do believe that every hardship can have a greater purpose and position us to impact others for the better. I don't think that my chubby, four-eyed, anxious middle school self would have jumped at the opportunity to go through what I did, but through that process I gained the ability to offer care and counseling to chronically and terminally ill patients and their families years later. The process may be hard, but the product is worth it.

POWERFUL STORIES

'AND ONCE YOU LIVE A GOOD STORY, YOU
GET A TASTE FOR A KIND OF MEANING
IN LIFE, AND YOU CAN'T GO BACK TO
BEING NORMAL; YOU CAN'T GO BACK TO
MEANINGLESS SCENES STITCHED TOGETHER
BY THE FORGETTABLE THREAD
OF WASTED TIME.'

DONALD MILLER

Good stories aren't flat, predictable, and prescribed. They have twists and turns, surprises, and even shocking moments that make the story that much better. Just like a good book, our lives are an ongoing narrative where characters develop, conflict gets faced head on, and resolution is reached towards the final pages of the book. For a powerful narrative to emerge from a season of struggle, we must be open to letting a plot twist occur. When we see suffering and challenges as something bigger, we step outside of our narrow, present vision to see it all playing a bigger role in the narrative of our lives. Hardships become woven into the tapestry to create powerful, unique stories. The challenges don't inhibit or define us; they simply create a better story.

We have the opportunity to see our failures as dead ends or we can choose to live a richer, fuller story.

From working with clients in therapy to engaging people across all socio-economic levels, we both encounter people living powerful stories. Many times, the most powerful stories are the unintended ones, like the mother now inspiring thousands of parents whose children have cancer after she lost her own son to cancer years ago. Or the recovering addict who now speaks encouragement to families staring into the dark hallways of their loved one's addiction. Or the therapist (Emily) whose own lifelong battle with anxiety has helped many of her clients struggling with anxiety disorders.

In America, we've been conditioned to want the ease of a predictable, carefree narrative without the excitement and thrill of unpredictable plot twists. If we want to live lives of happiness—lives that empower and inspire—we have to be willing to let go of the fantasy of a perfect ending we'll never have for the reality of a better story.

WE CAN'T SAVOR PRESENT BLESSINGS
WHEN CONSUMED WITH WHAT
WE THINK IS LACKING

Often we miss the goodness because we're clutching onto what we think we want while losing out on what could be an even better future. When life is hard, relationships get messy, and the path is unknown, we tend to get stuck trying to write our own perfect storyline.

Instead of comparing your current place in your story with the American Dream or someone else's happy ending, fight for purpose and keep perspective. Use the questions at the end of this chapter as an opportunity to heal, grow, and become more. When we own our stories and share them (the beautiful and messy stuff, too) we inspire others to do the same.

You were created to live for more than the status quo American Dream. *You* can use your past and current pain to live a greater story that frees others to do the same. You can change your happiness trajectory, but you have to choose to change.

The single biggest reason why things don't appear to change in our lives, especially when we face problems, is because we fail to change after facing those problems. If nothing changes within you, the exact same pain will emerge when you face the problem or pain again. Unless we change how we view or respond to a problem we will stay the same—and so will our story.

In most cases, people play the blame game instead of taking responsibility. They blame God or a Higher Power, other people, their boss, and their circumstances for their unhappiness. By no means are we suggesting every problem you face is completely in your control, but in all likelihood you have more power than you think you do to improve your circumstances. You can choose how you respond. And if we're being candid, you've contributed to many of the problems you face. Notice we did not say *all* or even *most*— but *many*. It's true for us as much as it is true for anyone. That might sting a bit to admit, but in our experience, it's the truth.

ANTHONY'S OUTLOOK

As I have matured through marriage and parenting, I've realized I am responsible for more of the problems I face with my wife and kids than I'd like to admit. How I engage them, my perception of *their* need to change, and *their* need to adapt to what's comfortable to me drives my emotional framework when engaging them. The result often isn't good.

But when I intentionally calibrate my perspectives when engaging them to keep my selfish tendencies in check, life is way more enjoyable for all of us. The more power I give their behaviors to govern my emotions, the more difficult it is for me to maintain joy, peace, and happiness. The issue is *me*, not them. The issue is *me*, not God. The issue is *me*, not those I work with.

It's a revolutionary thought really: I have the ability to choose my happiness. I have the ability to choose the level of joy and peace in my life. Regardless of the circumstances and situations around me, I can choose my emotional response to those conditions. The more I have accepted this reality in life, the more I have realized just how much power I have to choose happiness.

Remember where I'm coming from in life. I'm a guy who had all the odds stacked against him. I am still far from where I want to be, but I am also far from where I used to be. I challenge you this day to choose your emotions. Stop blaming circumstances, your workplace, friends, family, and even God for your work and life not turning out the way you wanted.

Take full responsibility for those areas where *you* let yourself down. You are the reason you didn't follow-through on that New Year's resolution, finish your undergraduate degree, start your Master's degree, start your business, get that promotion, have a successful marriage, become a committed father, terminate your addiction—or whatever else it may be. You let *yourself* down! It wasn't everyone else, it wasn't your circumstances, and it certainly wasn't God. Grow up. Take ownership of your unhappiness and start the process of doing whatever it takes to get to where you want to be. Find your Purpose. Then assess your coordinates—Family, Financial, Community, and Physical.

One thing you can know for sure—the blame game certainly won't get you there. The clock is ticking on your life. Every second you spend blaming is wasted energy that could be redirected toward the productive and healthy life you want to live. The road to happiness is the road less travelled, but I hope to see you on it. The choices that lie ahead in this book won't tell you where to go; they'll simply provide you with the option to choose your own happiness.

THE BOTTOM LINE

- Happiness isn't a set destination, but an active and ongoing process. It's something you *do*, not something you desire.
- Happiness is comprised of circumstances (both in and out of your control) and genetics.
- The road to character and personal development is just as important as the results. The process is just as important as the destination.
- *You* were created to live for more than the status quo American Dream. Use your past and current pain to live a greater story that frees others to do the same.

HAPPINESS NOW QUESTIONS

1. Do you believe happiness is a choice? Why or why not?

    _____

    _____

2. What stories encourage and inspire you in your journey?
    Consider all elements of their story, both the process
    and the end product. If it's possible, ask them what
    they would have told themselves while in the midst
    of the process to offer encouragement and additional
    perspective. Write these comments down so you can use
    them as insight in your daily life.

    _____

    _____

3. Think of your own story. What are some of your greatest
    accomplishments and joys in life? What challenges have
    helped paved the road to get you to this point. Write
    some of the situations down in the space below.

    _____

    _____

4. Do you spend too much energy allowing the circumstances around you to control your happiness? Why or why not?

_____

_____

5. What is your perspective on how much influence genetics, temperament, and other biological factors have on your natural responses to life's greatest challenges? With these influences in mind, consider what parts are in your control and what parts are not in your control. If possible, try to accept the things that are truly out of your control (this doesn't mean you have to appreciate or like them) and focus on improving the things that are in your control. We encourage reading the Serenity Prayer on a daily basis to help you in this process.

_____

_____

WHAT YOU SEE IS
WHAT YOU GET

"Everything can be taken from a man but one thing: the last of the human freedoms— to choose one's attitude in any given set of circumstances, to choose one's own way."

—Viktor E. Frankl, Jewish concentration camp survivor and psychologist

. . . .

BIG IDEA
Do you allow yourself to
dwell on negative thoughts?

. . . .

Think about the time in life when you were most satisfied and content. As we've pointed out already on our journey together, short-lived life circumstances don't make you happy. The initial excitement from a job promotion, first date, or buying a new house only lasts until the novelty wears off. These life events have value but when we think of the times you've felt most content, joyful, and at peace, it was probably a season of life that sounds relatively boring.

New York Times bestselling author and speaker Arthur Brooks says that the majority of things that make us truly happy are probably rather boring. Going on a long walk with your spouse, having a home-cooked family dinner on a Tuesday, or catching up with friends after being apart for many years are simple activities that produce deeply fulfilling outcomes. They aren't extravagant or noteworthy at the time, but they are life-giving and meaningful.

EMILY'S OUTLOOK

One of the most fulfilling times of life for me was in graduate school with a great group of counseling-student friends. I lived in a host home for free, drove an old car, and had very little money. My only job was as a part-time personal assistant picking up Christmas gifts and doing basic administrative work. None of us students had much money, so we did free stuff in Dallas—walks in the park, dance parties at someone's apartment, and free summertime concerts became truly priceless moments. We challenged one another, accepted one another, and grew in knowledge and together as human beings. There wasn't anything flashy about it, no life-changing situation, but we enjoyed the freedom of being fully known and fully loved. I call it my "Camelot season" and few seasons of life could ever compare. So how about you? What situation or season of life did you think of? How outrageous was it? Whatever situation came to mind, it most likely had some elements found in PERMA, Martin Seligman's theory of happiness and well-being. PERMA stands for Positive emotions, Engagement, Relationships, Meaning, and Accomplishments. If you cultivate these five areas, Seligman concluded, you will be happy. Think about it: the time in life when you felt most happy likely included some element of this model. Perhaps relationships thrived or you were working "in the zone," or were doing something that gave you a deep sense of meaning or accomplishment.

We've included a helpful chart (Figure 6.1) to illustrate the model. Seligman's model was groundbreaking and continues to be a popular one for seeing that happiness comes from more than one thing. While is it highly respected and helpful for the field of psychology, it might be a little

too abstract for most of us. That's why we prefer the 4 x 4
Happiness Model, which we will go into a bit later, with
the real-life coordinates we'll unpack shortly to help us all
achieve real-world happiness in life.

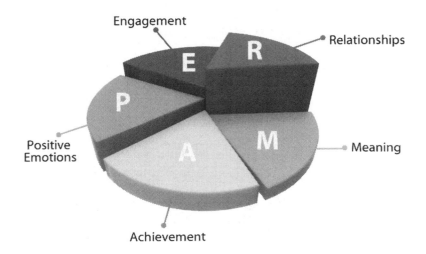

FIGURE 6.1 PERMA DIAGRAM
POSITIVE PSYCHOLOGY

The point is that whatever you did during that season you recall so fondly, it likely wasn't flashy or over the top. But it triggered positive feelings, which in turn reinforced a positive perspective on life that fueled more positive feelings. A study by Lyubomirsky, King, and Diener (2005) showed that positive feelings actually increase your chances of success in the first place. Their research revealed that happiness precedes successful outcomes and behaviors. In other words, not only *what you do*, but also *how you think* can position you to be happier. Seriously.

In other words, the person who gets a job promotion was probably happy *before* his title and salary changed. His positive mindset, resilience when facing challenges, and dedication to do his best made him stand out when his manager looked for a replacement before retirement. Now, to people on the outside, he may look happy because of his successes. But in reality, he became successful *because* he was happy, and not the other way around.

WHICH BRINGS US TO A SIMPLE TRUTH:
WHERE YOUR FOCUS GOES,
YOUR ENERGY FLOWS.

As Henry Ford put it, "Whether you think you can or can't, you're right." Your ability to achieve happiness is directly correlated to the perspective you choose to have, because what you see is what you get. Your happiness is directly related to your ability to make a conscious decision to choose. You can choose happiness, or you can choose unhappiness. You can choose how we see our opportunities and obstacles. You can choose to allow setbacks to hold you back, or you can choose to rebound from them.

New York bestselling author of *The Happiness Equation*, Neil Pasricha, promotes developing happiness in everyday life by cultivating healthy habits and mindsets.[13]

Act first and *then* the feelings follow. After reviewing hundreds of studies on the subject matter, Pasricha found that several happiness habits slowly shift our brain to becoming more positively focused and thus happier people. His "Big 7" includes taking three walks a week, writing for twenty minutes about positive experiences, five random acts of kindness, meditating, and five gratitude entries in a journal.

His ideas are supported by other research such as a study of Stanford students who reported a significantly higher level of happiness for those who engaged in at least five random acts of kindness weekly. The authors of the study, psychologists Richard Ryan, Veronika Huta, and Edward Deci, say that the productivity we create in meaningful lives and community is connected to our actively aiming to maximize happiness and decrease factors that cause pain.[14]

We agree with other experts that find meaning by imbuing the situation with meaning. Our perspective is what gives it the greatest value. Thus, any job can have meaning and fulfillment if we choose to focus on the outcomes such as building meaningful relationships at work, growing in our careers, or providing for our families. Meaning isn't found in the new job or raise, but rather in the mindset we have regarding our work.

Finding value and worth in your current position will lead to greater happiness than a change in your job title. How's that for an instant raise? Want to feel better about your life? Challenge the negative thoughts; turn the television and computer off to fully engage with your family. Want to meet a significant other? Make your life more interesting by engaging in new activities in new environments. See the difference for yourself by trying out our suggestion for a month. Note the difference it makes when you change your perspective.

ANTHONY'S OUTLOOK

When I faced a mountain of setbacks in life, I had plenty of opportunities to be upset or disappointed when confronted with major obstacles or hurdles in life. Statistically, I should have been down and out, but I chose a positive path. For example, I gave up my full football scholarship after only one semester to return home to finish college at The University of Memphis.

Only nine percent of kids from my background, according to the US Department of Education, ever finish a Bachelor's degree by the age of twenty-five. And getting an athletic scholarship is often the way many of those nine percent pay for it. So walking away from a football scholarship took my odds of success down even more.

However, I chose to rebound. Rather than focus on negativity or the long odds, I intentionally chose a positive mindset. I powered through my schoolwork and became Top Student in my major and continued after school to great success in business. But it all started because I made a choice to see things differently. And so can you.

EMILY'S OUTLOOK: CASE STUDY

Michelle was new to town and had recently graduated from pharmacy school. She graduated with high honors and had several job offers even before graduation day. Bright and driven with a hopeful future, Michelle had the unhealthy habit of overthinking every decision. Her analytical brain helped her solve complex problems and situations at work, but it was getting the best of her in her personal life.

She would ruin every romantic relationship she was involved in because she would overanalyze each date. She would obsess over what her dates said to the point where she'd project any minor nuance as being the key issue to potentially break up their possible marriage— twenty years in the future. Her ruminating over the negatives resulted in a pessimistic outlook about her future. Her perspective caused her to become hopeless and depressed. Her depression would cause her to act in ways that only reinforced her negative perspective. She became stuck in the cycle of negative feelings, which resulted in perfectly fine dates quickly going sour. To help Michelle, we focused on disengaging her from those negative automative irrational thinking patterns. She was given five minutes each day to write out her negative thoughts and worries—but only during that specific time. I then asked her to spend five minutes to write about the exact opposite—a positive outlook. Instead of thinking of the worst-case scenario, I asked to write about the best-case outcomes. Then we wrote down a realistic outcome. With all three options, she added potential healthy responses to the possible outcomes and ways to problem solve if they actually did happen. We looked at ways she could rationally respond and problem solve instead of overestimating negative outcomes and underestimating her ability to problem solve.

She needed to see the power of her thoughts and how her automatic negative thoughts hurt her more than the situations ever could. We worked on creating a "courtroom" for her negative thoughts. She wrote down the evidence that her negative thoughts were true and evidence that her negative thoughts were incorrect. She often discovered that her negative thoughts had very little evidence, yet she gave them her complete attention throughout the day.

Whenever she was tempted to ruminate on the negative, I provided a "tool kit" for her made up of a gratitude journal, serenity prayer, stress ball, and her favorite upbeat music. I encouraged her to go on a walk, which released endorphins in the brain to enhance her mood, talk with a friend about something completely unrelated, or watch a funny movie. She became active in her church's homeless outreach on a weekly basis, which helped her have a greater sense of purpose and gratitude in her own life as she served the less fortunate. By changing the way she thought and behaved, she was able to reduce her depression, anxiety, and hopeless mindset and begin to enjoy freedom once again.

HOW TO DEAL WITH NEGATIVE THOUGHTS

We can have healthy habits and do all the "right" things, but if we aren't being self-aware about our internal conversations, none of it will matter. What you think about, you bring about. If we only change the exterior, and not the inside thoughts, all we're doing is modifying behavior—and that won't be sustainable. Dwelling on negativity never empowered anyone to accomplish anything worthwhile. In fact, negative beliefs will often set you back more than the actual, real-life situations. When we speak to ourselves in a negative manner, we invite depression into our lives. We entertain the idea that we're not good enough, not smart enough, not capable of doing what we've set out to do when we ruminate on negativity. Negativity tells you you'll never succeed, but that's not true!

For example, Emily worked with one female professional to help her overcome a fear of public speaking. Just thinking about speaking would trigger panic attacks for this woman. But the worst part of it wasn't the event itself but the anxious, negative thoughts that bombarded her before the event and those that came afterwards, when she scrutinized every second of the presentation, convincing her that she had failed miserably. Left unchecked, those beliefs about herself would change her perspective about her ability to present, but even more so, her very identity and worth. They would limit future opportunities for growth and cost her in a big way. She would get stuck and never become what she could have become—not because she lacked ability, but because the negative beliefs would become so toxic and corrosive.

Likewise, Anthony's success in overcoming obstacles has been fueled primarily by a fighter mentality when it comes to taking control of the thoughts in his mind. He had no mentors or guides to help him figure out how to think. He heard negative talk in his home, so he chose to get intentional about changing the scripts in his mind. He has listened to podcasts, watched TED talks and other inspirational content, read hundreds of books, hung around wildly successful people, and saturated himself with positive thinking.

The self-talk change he made is why he is where he is today. For example, when tempted to worry, he intentionally chooses an alternative, positive option to think about rather than letting negative thinking win the day. He now recognizes the negative self-talk when it surfaces and combats it with something positive. Over time, his brain has bought into new patterns of thinking, because he genuinely believes the human mind does what we tell it to do. Let that truth sink in for a moment!

That's why he ends almost every email he sends with, "Make the day great!" This statement implies that you have the power to make it so. He had to rewire his brain and change his self-talk to get out of the pain and poverty of his past. And so must you to break whatever negative barriers are keeping you from choosing to live a more meaningful, fulfilling life.

Your brain is wired for survival, hence your natural fight-or-flight response. By thinking and acting confidently, your positive mindset can bring your feelings into reality. In most cases, unfortunately, we let our thinking respond to our emotions instead of the other way around. For example, when we're cut off in traffic, we feel offended and yell at the driver who can't hear a word we're saying and may not even know what just happened. How irrational is that? Yet we become slaves to that incident when we let our emotions take over instead of choosing how we want to respond. We react instead of realizing our own negative thought process and replacing it with positive thoughts. And what do we see the next time we hit the road? More drivers clearly intending to cut us off. Not surprisingly, what we tell ourselves we *will* see is what we *do* see. Our mind creates its own version of reality and then subconsciously brings it to life.

CHANGING YOUR SELF-TALK

Self-talk is a composition of the thoughts you affirm on a daily basis; oftentimes, they are so automatic and engrained, we don't even notice them unless we are trained to do so. They affect the overall outcome of your life and are, perhaps, the most critical determinant of your happiness. It is the most important piece of the realization process. All of us can close the gap between our destination—happiness—and our location—current reality—by taking control of our self-talk.

Zig Ziglar wrote an affirmation that he encouraged everyone to read every day to themselves while standing in front of the mirror. As Mr. Ziglar put it, "You are the most influential person you'll ever talk to." Emily regularly encourages her clients to do something similar. It begins with becoming aware of the self-talk you're already using.

We encourage you to get intentional about discovering the self-talk script playing in your head. Take a notebook with you throughout the day (or use a note taking app if that works better for you) and capture notes about the messages you're delivering to yourself. Think of it as a personal anthropological experiment. You can even speak of yourself in the third person if that helps. "Today, Emily reacted this way when she…. She thought this when the boss said…." You get the idea. Study yourself; because you can't change what you don't know exists. The more aware you become of how you think and act, the better you can test possible solutions.

Think of it like using the scientific method. Make observations about yourself and ask questions. Where does negative self-talk come from? What limiting beliefs are holding you back? Just as a train follows the rails, so your brain follows certain established patterns. To change the destination of your brain train, you have to switch tracks. You have to retrain your brain to reach a better destination. Listen within for the answers to your questions then make a hypothesis and a prediction based on that hypothesis. Then test it and assess the results to improve and test again. Try out different approaches to self-talk to discover the most effective conversations you need to have with yourself to close the gap.

Your brain can create new ways of thinking even when it doesn't fully buy into the new direction. By acting and talking "as if" your new, positive reality is already a done deal, you can train your brain to form new connections and position yourself for greater fulfillment in work and life. Because what you see really is what you get.

THE BOTTOM LINE

- The happiest moments are often simple but meaningful experiences with significant people.
- What you see is what you get. Your ability to achieve happiness is directly correlated to the perspective you choose to have.
- To close the gap between our destination—happiness— and our location—current reality—we have to change our negative self-talk.
- Any job can have meaning and fulfillment if you choose to focus on producing meaningful outcomes.

HAPPINESS NOW QUESTIONS

1. Arthur Brooks suggests that many happy moments in life aren't extraordinary or even notable to others. They're based upon the meaning and value ascribed to the situation by the people involved. When was the last time you experienced a satisfying and meaningful moment? Think of some ways you could cultivate a similar scenario in the coming month and assess the experience afterwards.

_____

_____

2. "Where your focus goes, your energy flows." Where does your focus go when you aren't actively engaged at work or in conversation? Ask yourself how your frame of thinking around happiness positively or negatively impacted your life.

_____

_____

3. Negative thinking about yourself, your situations, and future outcomes can become self-fulfilling prophecies.

Cognitive Behavioral Therapy, a specialized and respected type of psychotherapy, identifies negative thoughts as automatic, because they are often so habitual that we aren't even aware of them.

In the list below, identify the top three negative thought habits you find yourself using on a regular basis:

- **All-or-Nothing Thinking:** You see things in black-and-white categories. If your performance falls short of perfect, you see yourself as a total failure.
- **Overgeneralization:** You see a single negative event as a never-ending pattern of defeat.
- **Mental Filter:** You pick out a single negative detail and dwell on it exclusively so that your vision of all reality becomes darkened, like the drop of ink that discolors the entire beaker of water.
- **Disqualifying the Positive:** You reject positive experiences by insisting they "don't count" for some reason or other. In this way, you can maintain a negative belief that is contradicted by your everyday experiences.
- **Jumping to Conclusions:** You make a negative interpretation even though there are no definite facts that convincingly support your conclusion.

- **Mind Reading:** You arbitrarily conclude that someone is reacting negatively to you, and you don't bother to check this out.

- **The Fortuneteller Error:** You can anticipate that things will turn out badly, and you feel convinced that your prediction is an already-established fact.

- **Magnification (Catastrophizing) or Minimization:** You exaggerate the importance of things (such as your goof-up or someone else's achievement), or you inappropriately shrink things until they appear tiny (your own desirable qualities or other fellow's imperfections). This is also called the "binocular trick."

- **Emotional Reasoning:** You assume that your negative emotions necessarily reflect the way things really are: "I feel it, therefore, it must be true."

- **Should Statements:** You try to motivate yourself with should and shouldn't, as if you had to be whipped and punished before you could be expected to do anything. "Musts" and "oughts" are also offenders. The emotional consequences are guilt. When you direct *should* statements toward others, you feel anger, frustration, and resentment.

- **Labeling and Mislabeling:** This is an extreme form of overgeneralization. Instead of describing your error, you attach a negative label to yourself. "I'm a loser." Mislabeling involves describing an event with language that is highly colored and emotionally loaded.

- **Personalization:** You see yourself as the cause of some negative external event, which, in fact, you were not primarily responsible for.
- **Exercise:** Write out the situation or negative thought, and rate it from 1-10. Challenge the thought using the questions below, and write down a more realistic, positive response. Finally, identify your mood and rate it from 1-10.

If you struggle with negative thinking errors, try doing this exercise two to three times a day for ninety days. Write out your findings in a journal and reference it regularly.

4. Try these Challenge Questions:

- Am I falling into a thinking trap (e.g., *catastrophizing* or *overestimating danger*)?
- What is the evidence that this thought is true? What is the evidence that this thought is not true?

- Have I confused a thought with a fact? What would I tell a friend if he/she had the same thought? What would a friend say about my thought?
- Am I 100% sure that _____will happen? How many times has _____happened before?
- Is _____so important that my future depends on it?
- What is the worst that could happen? If it did happen, what could I do to cope with or handle it?
- Is my judgment based on the way I feel instead of facts? Am I confusing "possibility" with "certainty"? It may be possible, but is it likely?
- Is this a hassle or a horror?

Take a picture of this list for your own use and give to someone you respect so they can ask you when you feel overwhelmed or unable to be objective.

THE LIES WE'VE
BEEN TOLD

*"Happiness is not a goal...
it's a by-product of a life well lived."*

—Eleanor Roosevelt

....

BIG IDEA
What does the American
Dream mean to you?

....

Before we begin enabling your Life GPS and identifying your four key coordinates on the Happiness Map, we would be remiss if we didn't address the elephant in our cultural room—the American Dream. In the Declaration of Independence, we, as American citizens, affirmed our rights to life, liberty, and the pursuit of happiness. As settlers inhabited this land, they sought a better life, a place where greater freedom, education, and financial mobility would be possible. Owning property, building houses, and wealth became possible through hard work instead of being tethered to one's social class, race, or caste. As the land was inhabited, Americans worked for a better life for themselves and for the generations to follow. Their sacrifices were grounded in the belief that diligent effort and dedication could produce a better life for future generations.

This same mindset is still ingrained in us as Americans. Many parents today desire to offer their children opportunities they lacked in life. Unfortunately, it is easy to translate our altruistic ethos of our founders into something more egocentric and self-serving. Our ancestors worked long hours in hopes of establishing jobs for their families and community and to provide an easier path towards success for their children. Not that they didn't benefit themselves from the work, but they pursued something higher, nobler, and less selfish in many ways. You might even call it a value-driven capitalism that fueled our financial and cultural engine; as opposed to the crony capitalism we see so much of today.

As the years progressed, subsequent generations shifted from an agricultural, community-centered society to the more independent living of an industrial era. Long gone were the days where the family toiled together on the farm, where group-work and interdependence was expected, even required to stay alive. My, how the times have changed! Now, instead of fighting for freedom for all, farming for the good of the community, and engaging in intergenerational living, we obsess over selfies, getting more "likes" on social media, and other self-promoting avenues. And the change affects us all.

AN ENTITLED NATION

Just like the right to speak freely and vote, it's easy these days to believe that being happy and getting our slice of the American Dream are rights, as well. And we simply cannot imagine someone being unhappy after achieving that perceived American Dream. The two have become so intertwined—happiness and the American Dream—that we've all been conditioned that the more someone has, the happier they must be. The funny TV commercials, catchy print ads, and flashy billboards all tell the American consumer that life, liberty, and the pursuit of happiness is defined by having the latest and greatest—whatever.

If you don't believe us, test this theory for yourself when you watch commercials by asking, "What are they *really* selling?" They aren't selling a fast-food meal, they are selling the myth that if you buy the 1,000-calorie burger you will be as attractive, satisfied, and happy as the TV model appears to be while eating with other actors posing as one big happy family. It's a lie. None of that stuff brings happiness. We have both worked closely with people at both ends of the socioeconomic spectrum, from richest of the rich to the poorest of poor. We find them on what we call the *misery continuum* no matter how much or how little stuff they have.

Happiness can happen now, no matter what you do or do not have; it's determined primarily by the attitude we bring to the table. We can choose to be thankful for what we have, who we are, and where we are in the moment, or we can buy into the belief that "just a little bit more" will make us happy. When we hold to the latter, we believe that reaching our goals is the ultimate, most satisfying achievement. We put our successes on a pedestal and bow to them. Once we achieve the American Dream, we think we'll have fulfilling lives and satisfying relationships. But it doesn't work that way. Consequently, so many people climb the corporate ladder only to find that their ladder was leaning against the wrong building. They pour themselves into winning the rat race, and then realize they never wanted to be a rat in the first place.

This faulty way of thinking leaves little hope for those who haven't yet achieved their dreams. Yet this flawed belief hits us all—whether we live in subsidized housing or mansions. We can all be guilty of obsessing over whatever the "next" big dream is that is supposed to bring happiness. The lie creates a faulty belief based on the *if this, then that* paradigm we discussed earlier. *If* we have more _____, *then* we will be happy. This lie turns the American Dream into the American Myth, and we hear it all the time. "If I have a bigger house, my kids will be happier. If I have more money, I'll be happier because I can buy more stuff." The American Myth degrades happiness as nothing more than a passive byproduct of wealth, success, and materialistic gains.

> IN REALITY, WE CAN HAVE MONEY AND STILL NOT BE HAPPY, AND WE CAN BE HAPPY WITHOUT MONEY.

Character development, emotional well-being, and mutually beneficial relationships can exist where financial success and achievements do not. While money and achievement do allow for greater flexibility and opportunities, they do not produce ongoing happiness and perfection. The roof to that "perfect house" leaks, the cute puppy pees on the Oriental rug, and the romantic date night with your spouse gets indefinitely postponed for little league games and gymnastic meets. Life happens!

The American Dream is nothing more than an ideal; that's it. When we believe the American Dream will provide fulfillment, we put too much weight into the dream and lose sight of how we can be happy in the midst of unanswered prayers and "not yet" seasons. Setting a goal to be happy is wonderful, but the belief that happiness is found in achievement, materialism, or any person is, ironically, the greatest barrier to real happiness.

EMILY'S OUTLOOK: CASE STUDY

A middle-aged mother of two teen girls, Caroline came into my office depressed. She had come from a poor family. Her dad was a mechanic and her mom worked as a waitress, working the night shift after her husband came home to watch the kids. One night, a fight escalated between two customers. Guns were drawn and Caroline's mom was killed in the crossfires. At twelve years old, Caroline had to step into her mom's shoes for her three younger siblings and her father, who never really recovered from the loss.

With tears in her eyes, she recounted days where she'd never see her father and then hear him stumble in late, drunk, yelling, and breaking dishes. She'd find him passed out on the sofa as she prepared the other kids' school lunches in the morning. He died the weekend of her high school graduation. He had downed a bottle of Jack Daniels and driven into a median.

To say Caroline's past was painful would be an understatement. Twelve is too young to grow up so fast. She remembered seeing families on television that seemed so happy. She wanted to have a family that looked like them. She shared, "I thought that if I worked hard in school, I could earn scholarships that could open doors for college. I could find a nice guy who would marry me and provide me with the life I always wanted. Maybe my life was a nightmare now, but I could be like the moms in those shows where the husband is happy to come home and the kids' biggest fears are the monsters under the bed or not being asked to prom."

With this fantasy in mind, Caroline grabbed the first guy she could find. They quickly married the weekend after they graduated from college. She became pregnant only a few months later, just as he started medical school. She wanted a stable, predictable, and safe life, but when she actually had that stability, she only experienced severe emptiness and self-doubt.

As time went on, her children complained about the clothes they didn't have. They struggled in school because they lacked the motivation to study. Her husband was rarely home due to the demands of his growing medical practice. She had the big house, the kids, and the successful husband, but behind closed doors she was deeply depressed and disappointed by the emptiness of it all.

Facing the failure of her American Dream, she confessed, "My friends don't know me, my husband doesn't pursue me, and my kids only tolerate me when they want money to shop. I spent my life creating a picture of what I thought life should be, but no one said how lonely it can actually be." Caroline, traumatized by her painful childhood, believed that an American Dream checklist would satisfy and offer a happy, fulfilling life. She saw it as a way to transform her life from a living nightmare to a euphoric dream.

She had become overly dependent upon other people and looked to them to make her feel better about herself and more satisfied with life. She had bought into the American Myth, thinking that if she could just achieve it, all would be well. It wasn't, and that reality left her deeply discouraged. Through therapy, she recognized the unrealistic expectations she had placed on her family and possessions. She began realizing how healing from past wounds, creating meaningful relationships, and creating a greater sense of self would bring far more happiness than any American Myth could ever do.

Clients like Caroline have allowed me to see that what we expect and even demand can get in the way of what we really need to be happy. The American Myth was only a mirage she was chasing. It was only after she released herself from her unrealistic timeline, demands, and expectations of herself and others, that she was able to fully heal from her trauma, make peace with the past, embrace her beautiful blessings in life, and truly find happiness.

ANTHONY'S OUTLOOK

Anyone who believes the alleged American Dream has always been, and is currently accessible to all people, is dreaming! We are blown away by the number of people who suggest "hard work" alone will cure poverty. Poverty is a learned behavior, which in many cases is inescapable unless someone not living in poverty steps in, advocates on behalf of the impoverished, and guides people to a better place. Why would anyone expect the impoverished to know anything other than poverty?

Show us people who are convinced hard work alone got them to a position of success, and we will show you people full of misconception and arrogance. Newsflash: you didn't get to where you are alone. The money you earn, the cars you drive, the roads you drive on, the computers you use, the wireless system you use, the company you work for, or even the company you built came to you because of some type of connection with others. Ultimately, we all have the privilege of benefiting from the labor of others.

If you have been blessed with opportunity, quit whining about what you don't have and focus on what you do have. Then start setting your happiness coordinates for the journey and reach out to take others with you on the journey. Find someone who lacks opportunity and invite him or her to come along. Don't give a handout. Offer a hand up and just see how helping someone else succeed affects your own level of happiness.

THE BOTTOM LINE

- Happiness can happen now, no matter what you do or do not have; it's determined primarily by the attitudes you bring to the table.
- The American Myth degrades happiness as nothing more than a passive byproduct of wealth, success, and materialistic gains.
- While money and achievement do allow for greater flexibility and opportunities, they do not produce ongoing happiness and perfection.
- The belief that happiness is found in achievement, materialism, or any person is the greatest barrier to real happiness.

HAPPINESS NOW QUESTIONS

1. How do you define *The American Dream*?

_____

_____

2. How has your upbringing influenced your thoughts on happiness and how you define *The American Dream*?

_____

_____

3. What do you insert in the *if this, then that* paradigm? Think about what you've inserted in this paradigm in the past and consider whether it proved to be productive and helpful.

_____

_____

4. It may be helpful to imagine what someone from a different socioeconomic group, race, or gender would insert in the *if this, then that* paradigm.

5. What one thing do you intend to change regarding your perspective on happiness and its direct correlation to accumulating stuff?

_____

_____

PURPOSE:
ENABLING YOUR GPS

"The place God calls you to is the place where your deep gladness and the world's deep hunger meet."

—*Frederick Buechner*

. . . .

BIG IDEA
Are you clear on your purpose?

. . . .

Y our navigation device in your car won't do you any good unless you turn it on. The same is true with our 4 x 4 Happiness Model. Put simply, your Life GPS must be enabled before use.

Think about it. Suppose you knew your coordinates, you knew how to find north, south, east, and west, but had no clue where you wanted to go? What good would it do you? So it is with the Happiness Coordinates. Before you get clear on your coordinates in the chapters that follow, you need to enable your GPS—find your higher purpose in life. Without it, you'll drift aimlessly and end up somewhere that doesn't resemble happiness at all.

Everything has a purpose—even the pain in your past mentioned earlier. We all have pain in our lives, but harnessing it appropriately allows us to change the narrative. If used effectively, pain can push us to find a clearer purpose in life. We can redeem it and use it for good rather than letting it destroy us.

For example, Emily grew up surrounded by medical issues and pain from trauma, and it drove her to want to help other people. She had the choice to let the pain destroy her or to use it to help other people. Likewise, Anthony experienced the pain of poverty, severe insecurities, self-doubt, and verbal abuse. He dealt with bullies in the hood, overt racism in middle and high school, and trash-talking peers. He instinctively fought his way past the pain—literally. Fortunately, playing football gave him a legal and controlled channel to "kindly" share his frustrations through high-velocity collisions—and he took full advantage of it. Pushing past the pain earned him a college football scholarship to play with some of the best talent in the world. He chose to channel his pain toward finding a way out of his circumstances and improving his life. So can you.

GETTING SERIOUS ABOUT BEING HAPPY

You may recall that the Gallup-Sharecare Well-Being Index also discovered that the most common trait shared by happy people was having a clear sense of purpose in life. Happiness is no accident.

> HAVING A CLEAR SENSE OF DIRECTION IN LIFE
> EMPOWERS YOU TO PUT LIFE IN CONTEXT
> AND SETBACKS IN PERSPECTIVE

If all we have to guide us are day-to-day events, we're sure to end up somewhere we don't want to go—and probably miserable.

Both of us rely heavily on our faith to identify our life purposes, but you don't have to share our Christian faith to recognize the need to see meaning beyond the day-to-day world. When we don't have a broader perspective on life—and our place in it—we tend to see the world from a self-centered perspective that quickly leaves us feeling ungrateful and filled with anxiety about what might happen next. Dealing with life purpose means we have to come to grips with what we believe about the big questions in life. Consequently, some people would rather leave their Life GPS turned off. Those questions about vision and purpose don't go away, even though we may hide behind excuses.

One of the biggest excuses we hear is related to time: *I don't have time to figure out my life purpose.* If that's true, why have so many other successful people gotten clear on their purpose and accomplished their goals? They have the same twenty-four hours all of us have. It's not about how much time you have; it's what you do with the time you have that counts.

Time is constant for all of us. The only variable that changes is you. If you don't have time to find your direction, you'll be wasting even more time floundering every day.

YOU SEE, MOST OF US DON'T HAVE
A TIME MANAGEMENT ISSUE; WE HAVE
AN ENERGY MANAGEMENT ISSUE.

Because we don't have a clear purpose, we don't focus our energy on the best things. Bottom line: you don't need to manage *time*. You need to manage *you*.

Self-management begins with getting clear on your purpose. Once you have that, you can discipline yourself and create a structure that allows you to fulfill your purpose and achieve your goals in the four coordinate areas and more.

The first step to getting clear on your purpose is to stop and take a step back. Most of us have been trained to think by institutions—elementary, middle school, high school, and college structures. Most of us simply follow the conventional path, never questioning why or if that path is right for us. We simply go with the flow and follow well-meaning parents, peers, and cultural influences, then don't like where we end up. But it doesn't have to be that way.

A friend of ours, we'll call him Henry, started to pursue his passion for videography as a young man. But then he was convinced that a more conventional path to success should take him to medical school. He became a well-paid surgeon primarily because he listened to what others told him to do rather than figuring out his own life direction. Everything changed for Henry, however, when he was introduced to a motivational speaker who needed videography help. Henry took a step back and reevaluated his life direction. He stepped away from performing surgery on people and started performing surgery on video. He now loves what he does so much that his wife has to help him turn it off at the end of the day!

Henry's true purpose was in video production, but he listened to the voices of the people around him. He is not alone. How many musicians went to law school instead of following their passions? How many corporate CEOs would have preferred to be educators, but followed the career path laid out before them instead? How many people in corporate America are disengaged in the workplace because they're afraid to discover their purpose and see if a better fit exists within their present company?

WHERE TO START

We suggest you start to get clear on your purpose by listing some of your non-negotiable things in life. Are there faith factors or beliefs that mean a lot to you? List those as big rocks. Are family relationships key? Put those down. What are the talents and skill sets you really want to develop? Do you have passions you've been longing to pursue? Is there a position in your company that you've been eying for a while but lacked the courage to go for it? As the old saying goes, if you don't know where you want to go, any old road will get you there.

Psychologists talk about having an internal and external locus of control. A person who has an internal locus of control believes he or she can influence and control events and outcomes. Someone with an external locus of control blames external items and people for everything. If you live with an external locus of control mindset, you become your own greatest enemy.

You have more power to change than you think. Even in the most extreme cases, we have power to control how we respond to circumstances. The issue is not whether or not we actually have the power, but coming to believe that we do have the power. For example, do you hate cold weather? Move to a warmer climate. If you live in Green Bay, Wisconsin and hate the cold, move south if warmer weather means a better quality of life. In the same way, you have permission to identify other things in your life that can contribute to your joy—and pursue them.

Once you've listed what you want, align it with where you're at right now—your education, experience, knowledge, skills, etc. How can you leverage where you are to get where you want to go?

Do you need to grow your leadership capacity, acquire new skills, or relocate to get there?

Next, begin thinking about what types of careers paths or careers tracks in your organization would best align with your purpose.

After you brainstorm and exercise due diligence, you can begin building a strategic and accountable plan that, if executed well, will get you where you want to go.

Keep in mind, that maintaining the status quo has benefits. If you keep drifting, you won't have to do the hard work of change. It's convenient to stay right where you are. It takes effort to push past the pain of growth. A lot of people talk about *being* intentional but never *do* anything intentional.

PEOPLE DON'T JUST DO WHAT THEY SAY—
THEY DO WHAT THEY VALUE.

Use the resistance to change your encounter to motivate you to make positive changes in your life. Turn your growth pains into purpose gains.

One thing we strongly recommend is that you complete the process by creating a purpose statement, a short summary of what you want your life purpose to be. Write it down. Put it somewhere where you will review it often and regularly affirm it. Emily's purpose statement, for example, is to allow others to experience the safety and freedom necessary to become increasingly more and more the person they were made to be in the time we share together. Anthony's purpose statement is to add value to others through writing, speaking, coaching, and consulting.

We encourage you to engage the process and push back the fears to find the clarity you need. Discover your purpose and move forward with confidence.

EMILY'S OUTLOOK: BELIEF AND PURPOSE

In my years of mental health care, I've helped countless people trying to find their place in the world and identify the purpose in the pain. I've journeyed with parents through the loss of their young children to cancer, sat with teen girls as they heal from assaults and heartbreak that cut deeper than any physical wounds, and witnessed the beautiful picture of redemption when a wayward young adult beats her addiction and claims sobriety. In spite of the severity, situation, and specifics, everyone asks a common question: *Why?*

Sometimes it's the initial question. Sometimes it's tucked deep down in the soul, only to come out when triggered by overwhelming grief. Sometimes, it's barely a faint whisper in the darkness, doubting anyone will answer. I've heard, "Why, God?" hurled towards the heavens as if to gain the attention of a distant and distracted God. I've also heard it as the only recognizable words between all the wailing and tears. Regardless of the circumstances, the desire is the same, because we all want to know, especially in the face of heartache and sadness, that there's a purpose behind it all. We want reassurance that all is not in vain.

But, if I can just be candid, I really wonder if people need an answer to this question as much as they simply need comfort, reassurance, and validation. The mother who lost her son doesn't need a quick answer, because even if it could be offered, it wouldn't take away her pain. During those times, we need someone to sit with us in our pain, offer support, and simply express grief. No reason will ever be enough for some of the pain experienced in life. If I can lean into my own Christian faith for a moment, when were any of us ever promised all the answers in life? We're not guaranteed answers, but we are guaranteed we each only have one life to live. Why not make it one of purpose and fulfillment rather than becoming one mired in regrets?

My own faith in God persuades me that God will work all things towards the good. But He never promised life would be easy for any of us. Even Jesus himself wept at the news of tragedy and showed compassion for those He knew He would heal. In my opinion, those who walk away from their faith when life doesn't work out the way they want, only do so because they believe a God that doesn't exist in the first place owes them something He never promised.

Hard times can help you lean into your faith—a critical part of our bigger picture perspective on life. In the face of life's mountains, my friend Bill Blankschaen puts it this way in *A Story Worth Telling*:

Mountains make the ideal setting for the best stories.... Our natural inclination is to run from mountains, to flee from adversity, to take shelter when we see a storm brewing on the trail ahead. But faith focused on God moves us to walk toward the mountain in spite of the fear, to lean into the challenge—not so we can be proven great, but so that God can reveal himself on our behalf. It is only when we first move toward the mountain that God moves. Our motion is evidence of our devotion.[15]

In challenging situations, we discover God's true character—and ours—unlike any other time. Perhaps a story of someone working through struggles to a clear sense of purpose will help bring the need for purpose to life.

LAUREN'S STORY

Lauren had a surprisingly hard life for being so young. After a challenging childhood, she grew up quickly after marrying at nineteen. Six months into the marriage, she found out about her husband's same-sex interest. This led to divorce just four months later. After six years, Lauren remarried. She became pregnant soon afterwards and received little help from her husband. From his premature birth, the baby had health issues. Lauren became the primary caretaker while the father had an affair and ultimately left her for another woman. Not too long after the divorce, she got the call from her son's doctor: cancer. The prognosis wasn't good.

Lauren didn't know what to do. I encouraged her to call her "team" to meet at my office for her next appointment. Her team was a small group of women who were dedicated to walking beside her as she faced this battle. In that hour, I saw six young moms with hearts full yet broken. They wanted to help but they knew they were severely limited in what they could offer. We gathered around her, placed our hands on her, and prayed over this sweet young lady.

I reminded them of the Biblical account of challenges faced by the Israelites. After leaving bondage in Egypt and wandering in the desert for forty years, they were finally making progress. There was one problem—the Jordan River. During the rainy season when they arrived, the river could be up to a mile wide and about 150 feet deep. They had to choose to wait for a better season for crossing or, quite literally, step out and trust God. When they trusted, the waters dried up, allowing around a million people to pass through. They stacked stone from the river to remind them of God's faithfulness.

In my little counseling office, we didn't see God dry up any large bodies of water, but we did recall God's past faithfulness in Lauren's life. One by one, she and her friends recalled what God had done. They gathered around her and created stones. Their children actually collected stones, and the moms wrote events and dates for each event where God had been faithful. These stones rested on her mantel as a reminder of a larger purpose for her when her son's body rejected treatment after treatment and when he ultimately passed. The same God that guided the Israelites through the Jordan River, the same God that protected Lauren during a childhood trauma years ago, was the same God who walked with her through her son's cancer treatment and her grief journey. Her faith gave her a strong and steady sense of purpose through an extremely painful season of life.

The same can be true for you, too. I encourage you to consider times when pain has produced profound purpose. Write the events and dates down, or, better yet, do what Lauren did and write this information on rocks for you to view often. It's important to remember powerful stories when you find yourself in the midst of trials and suffering.

APPLYING YOUR 4 FULFILLMENT FACTORS

No matter your faith distinguishers, your purpose gives you direction in life. Without direction, each of us will flounder, being tossed along the trail by whatever comes our way. No wonder so many of us aren't happy. We end up in places we never wanted to be with no clue how to get somewhere better. But it doesn't have to be that way for you.

We invite you to embrace the simple process we described above and start your happiness journey right by getting clear on your core coordinate—purpose. Begin by applying the 4 Fulfillment Factors below to get the clarity you need to move to a happier, more fulfilling place.

THE BOTTOM LINE

- Having a clear sense of direction in life empowers you to put life in context and setbacks in perspective.
- People don't just do what they say—they do what they value.
- Harnessing pain appropriately allows you to change the narrative.
- Pain, once dealt with, will always provide a greater sense of purpose. Steward your pain wisely to produce the greatest purpose possible!
- Self-management begins with getting clear on your purpose.
- You don't need to manage *time*. You need to manage *you*.

HAPPINESS NOW QUESTIONS

Destination: Where Do I Want to Go?

1. What current dreams do I believe will support my journey toward happiness?

   _____

   _____

2. What is my big-picture goal for happiness?

   _____

   _____

Location: Where Am I Now?

1. Now that I'm halfway through the book, my happiness barometer on a scale of 1 to 10 (10 being outstanding) is _____.

2. Where would my closest family members suggest I am on that 1 to 10 scale? _____

3. Where would my close friends, peers and/or co-workers suggest I am on that 1 to 10 scale? _____

Realization: What Do I Need to Change to Close the Gap?

1. What two or three internal things can I change immediately to empower me to move toward my happiness destination?

   _____

   _____

2. What two or three external things within my control can I change immediately to empower me to move toward my happiness destination?

   _____

   _____

3. What two or three tools and/or resources do I need to use to empower me to move toward my happiness destination?

   _____

   _____

Acceleration: How Can I Best Move Forward Consistently?

1. What type of accountability structures do I need in my life to help me move toward my happiness destination? For example: having a board of directors, using organization apps, etc.

   _____

   _____

2. Who could be on my personal board of directors? Who are the best people in my life to help guide and encourage me along the path in the direction of happiness?

   _____

   _____

3. What do I anticipate might be the potential distractions and barriers to success as I move toward my desired state of happiness?

   _____

   _____

COORDINATE 1: FINANCES—MONEY, MONEY, MONEY

"Money never made a man happy yet, nor will it. There is nothing in its nature to produce happiness. The more a man has, the more he wants. Instead of filling a vacuum, it makes one."

—Benjamin Franklin

....

BIG IDEA
What financial security do you need to live your dream?

....

Once you are clear on your purpose, you can look at the four happiness coordinates to see how well they align with your intended direction. Until you know where you're going, the four coordinates really won't matter. But once you do have clarity of purpose, you can turn your attention to the first coordinate: financial.

We discuss financial first because in our experience. It's often the most prominent one people struggle with when trying to find fulfillment at work, which then affects happiness at home and the rest of life.

> 'SHOW ME A PERSON WHO BELIEVES MONEY
> IS THE ANSWER TO ALL OF LIFE'S PROBLEMS
> AND I'LL SHOW YOU A PERSON THAT HAS
> NEVER HAD A LOT OF MONEY!'
>
> UNKNOWN

This first Happiness Coordinate—Financial—is important to your happiness but not because money provides happiness. If you do what you love and manage your finances well, you'll position yourself to be happy. Money is simply a tool. You have the power to choose how you use it— hopefully, well.

We've both worked with people from all socioeconomic backgrounds, from the mega-wealthy to those mired in poverty. There's one truth we have found about people no matter how much or how little money they have: they're all equal candidates for misery. In other words, how much money they have has little to do with how happy they feel. Money doesn't buy happiness. We all know this reality somewhere in the back of our minds, and yet we still chase it as if it will somehow be different for us, as if we are the exception to the rule.

ANTHONY'S OUTLOOK: CAREERS

I have lived this reality in ways most professionals have not. I remember it as if it were yesterday. I went home to Memphis to have what I knew would be a tough conversation with my mother and stepfather. I had decided to walk away from my "dream job" at 3M, a Fortune 100 giant. As I expected, both of them told me it was the dumbest thing I had ever done. "Anthony, that's stupid!" my mother "lovingly" told me. "Why would you quit that job and leave all that money on the table? You can pursue ministry and motivational speaking anytime."

It wasn't easy, and it's not the right life path for everybody, but I was convinced walking away from the career path I spent my whole life trying to attain was the right step to make. Here I was, positioned to be the poster child for "making it out of the hood" and, not only was I walking away from money, but I was also headed into the non-profit world. No wonder everyone thought I was crazy.

At twenty-three, I had the responsibility of a four-state territory with all the corporate perks, bells, and whistles—healthy car allowance, expense account, the freedom to create my own schedule, and unlimited possibilities for financial gains. I have no doubt I would have made millions long-term and been in executive leadership at a Fortune 100 company.

One problem: I wouldn't have been happy because my financial coordinate would not have aligned with my purpose. That's not to say my financial path should be yours—not at all. You can be very happy matriculating through the ranks of traditional corporate America if that financial perspective aligns with your life purpose. It must do so if you aspire to be happy. Had I stayed the course, I'd probably be divorced, money would still be a god to me, my kids would probably not know me that well, and I'd still be trying to figure out why I love who I am on the outside but despise myself on the inside.

Because of the work I now do on a daily basis, both in the for-profit and non-profit space, I have the privilege of connecting with a lot of people from all walks of life. In my experience, the average person is desperately looking for a change of direction in life but feels overwhelmed by the financial risk of pursuing his or her dream. They spend a large portion of their lives working, but the intrinsic return on results is minimal and miserable.

One of my board members at The Gifted Foundation, who at the time of this writing serves as a Senior Business Consultant for Gallup, told me their research found 71% of employees are disengaged or unsatisfied with their current work culture.[16]

But how much of that frustration do those people bring with them to work each day because they feel they're simply working for a paycheck, health benefits, stock options, and a 401k?

I am not suggesting these things are insignificant. Quite the contrary. I realize the importance of financial security; however, I am puzzled by how many people are convinced their passions and dreams are unattainable. Consequently, they don't try to pursue them either with a career change or in parallel to their core work focus.

Self-starters who make a conscious decision every single day to do something they enjoy drive the American economy. They take ownership for their current role and step up to lead within their organization. They step out to start a new side venture or find a new career path that is better aligned with their purpose. Those who have the will, skill, and freedom from institutionalized thinking can create a new life if they choose to do so—as long as they are clear on their purpose.

But let's be candid: the problem for most people at work is that they would rather "clock in" every day and benefit from the sweat equity, risk, responsibility, stress, and productivity of others. For the average person, the pain of remaining the same does not outweigh the pain of change. This pain paradox is the key reason why so many people are unhappy at work. They want to drift and they want the benefits of stepping up. It doesn't work that way.

MONEY AND HAPPINESS

We're both convinced people are far more productive when they are engaged, excited, and fulfilled when they wake up in the morning. Both of us experience that every day and hope you do—or will soon. Don't let fears about money, whatever they might be, continue to hold your life purpose hostage. Live the life *you* are inspired to live.

A recent *Money* magazine article entitled "The Only 3 Things You Need to Know about Money and Happiness" reveals something fascinating on the subject. Researchers from The University of British Columbia and Michigan State University discovered that money can *decrease* sadness, but it cannot ultimately *increase* joy. In other words, the greatest advantage that people with disposable income have over those that do not is their ability to better navigate adversity or difficult circumstances:

A leaking roof might be annoying for a few days if you're rich, but a months-long ordeal that can cripple you physically, financially, and emotionally if you're poor. Makes sense, right?[17]

ANTHONY'S OUTLOOK

I have found this to be very true personally and of those with whom I work. Remember, I lived in a bug-infested apartment community for almost a decade as a child. I get it: life is a whole lot better with the ability to pay for pest control. When I had to deliver eulogies for my maternal grandmother, maternal grandfather, and stepfather, I experienced a sadness money could not resolve.

Now, I work alongside wealthy businesspeople as clientele. I have never met a wealthy person who didn't have at least one problem their money could *not* solve. In fact, every single person I know who has more than enough money also has more than enough problems. Money can't cure cancer, give an infertile mother a natural childbirth, mend a broken heart, satisfy an emotional gap in a stale marriage, or bring back a lost loved one.

Yet, even though we all know this to be true, so many of us still pour our time, energy, and heart's desire into chasing money. While having great wealth can reduce sadness and the struggle for daily survival to some extent, it cannot increase happiness. People addicted to the pursuit of wealth will find themselves trying to fulfill an ever-increasing desire with an ever-decreasing ability to satisfy.

WHY ENOUGH IS NEVER ENOUGH

Accomplished journalist Maia Szalavitz speaks to the issue of why enough is never enough:

While stereotypes suggest that poor people are more likely to lie and steal, new research finds that it's actually the wealthy who tend to behave unethically. In a series of experiments—involving everything from dangerous driving to lying in job negotiations and cheating to get a prize—researchers found that, across the board, richer people behaved worse. But, rather than class itself, the authors suggest that it's views about greed that may largely explain the difference.[18]

While some people cast stones at the less fortunate who appear to live their entire lives robbing Peter to pay Paul, we argue that many of the wealthy do the same. Greed is corrosive, no matter where it is found. For example, consider the 2008 economic downturn. While there were clearly multiple causes, the collapse of the Lehman Brothers financial firm tilted the entire global financial structure in the wrong direction. Many years before the crisis occurred, irresponsible financiers loaned a lot of money to irresponsible and/or incapable borrowers in the subprime mortgage lending space.

Almost anyone with poor credit history could secure a home loan, even though bankers knew it might be difficult, if not impossible, to repay the loan. Yet, the greed of these supposedly intelligent lenders inspired them to pool loans together and label them as low-risk securities. They assumed they could lower the risk of a single default by pooling high-risk loans together. It didn't work out well for either the lender or the lendee.

No one seemed to consider what might happen if the majority of the team were no longer able to carry the weight. That is exactly what happened and led to the crisis. All the payers collaborated to make the scheme work in the pursuit of more money, regardless of the best and highest purpose for the nation, the borrowers, or the lenders. The blind were leading the blind.

Imagine this *hypothetical* conversation:

Big Banks: "We're going to give mortgages to people who cannot afford to pay them. We will simply pool them all together, create Collateralized Debt Obligations (CDO's) and allow people to invest in them depending upon their credit rating. Credit Rating Agencies, will you please grade them on a curve because we don't want people to know they're really not worth what we're suggesting they're worth?"

Credit Rating Agencies: "Sure. Since you are the ones paying us, we'll rate them however you want. As you continue to rake in money from those who invest in these CDOs, you can pay us more money. And we will continue raising the bar on the ratings. How does that sound?"

Big Banks: "Great! The average person doesn't have the knowledge or the power to stop us from doing what we are doing, so no one will ever know. Those who do know will ignore it because it will ultimately benefit them also, even if only temporarily. Oh, and let's just keep this between us!"

Credit Agencies: "We won't tell if you don't tell!"

Big Banks: "Besides, we are too big to fail, so the government and taxpayers will just bail us out anyway if this scheme collapses."

Credit Agencies: "Sounds like a plan!"

We all know what happened next. The greed and stupidity of supposedly intelligent people were exposed. The collapse was proof that the most intelligent and seemingly successful people in the world are just as susceptible to greed and making stupid decisions when it comes to money as anyone else. If it were not for wealthy and poor taxpayers providing massive bailouts, I am not so sure we would have escaped the worst recession in more than eighty years.

ANTHONY'S OUTLOOK: GREED KILLS

Regardless of where you are financially, greed is ever-present. One of my very best friends from elementary school is doing life plus forty-seven years in prison for a gang-related murder and armed robbery. Yep, that's right. After he's dead from his life sentence, he still owes the system forty-seven more years. He was greedy. He broke into the home of a supposed friend and held him up. Gunfire ensued and my ex-friend ended up taking the life of the person he aimed to rob.

My former neighbors in middle and high school had a family of five boys and one girl. Several of the boys were locked up due to money-related crimes and the girl married a guy who somehow managed to grow a successful company almost overnight. Because he came from *the hood*, he operated the business with the same mentality he often saw there. He and his business partners made a lot of unethical decisions. They grew their real estate company swiftly and made millions of dollars in the residential and commercial real estate space. But he was eventually indicted on federal fraud charges, sentenced to decades in prison, and ordered to pay millions of dollars in restitution.

Once again, greed was at the center of it all. The moral of all these stories is that if you don't control your love of money, it will control you. It can take you places you never imagined and inspire you to do things you never thought you would do. Allowing the spirit of greed to run your life will keep you from ever achieving your purpose and finding fulfillment. You'll drift off course and end up shrugging your shoulders, unable to explain how you got to such an unfulfilling place. **Greed is the silent killer of happiness!**

WHAT TO DO ABOUT IT

Sadly, we know a lot of people who make a significant amount of money in their careers yet would do anything to trade seats with us in order to experience the joy we know on a daily basis. As a nation, we don't just have a spending problem, we have self-medicating problem with money. Think about it. If we have $100 bill in our wallets but the clothes or that online gadget costs $150, we cannot afford to pay cash for it. But, instead of telling ourselves that we cannot afford to buy the item, we self-medicate with our ubiquitous credit cards. Just like emotionally eating when going through a stressful time or break up, many Americans use their credit cards as maladaptive coping devices, consuming to fill up the painful voids. Overspending is a way we try to mask, numb, or deal with underlying emotional issues.

We might buy items because we had a hard day and feel like we deserve it, because our kids have been in a mood all week and this might brighten their day, or because our friends have one and we want to be like them. Whatever the reason, it certainly isn't a logical one. Being happy in our finances means that we don't use our money (items) to fix emotional impulses, voids, and problems.

The way to be happiest with money is not to look to it to provide happiness. After reading our stories in this chapter, we think you get this message loud and clear. We encourage you to be wise with your finances, not to "buy happiness" but to be financially stable and secure for whatever comes in the future. Buying a new outfit, new car, or going out to the overpriced fancy restaurants is sexy and exciting in the moment. Saving, budgeting, and creating financial plans are not in the moment. Don't get us wrong, there's nothing wrong with buying things when you have the money to back those purchases. When you don't have the money, you'll go into greater debt or feel the stress of making monthly payments from an already overstretched bank account. **Delayed gratification is critical to experiencing real joy in life.** Discipline and sacrifices are required on the front end of life to experience the greatest joy you can possibly imagine in later years.

Now don't misunderstand us: money can be a tool to help you become happier when used wisely. According to Sierra Black, by spending your money on experiences rather than items, you tend to have happier feelings and memories toward your purchases.[19] Your memories of your experiences last forever while "stuff" does not. But there is a limit to how much happiness money can actually buy. The more money you receive reduces your negative emotions— but only to a point. A study showed that around $70,000 per year per individual is the best income to reduce negative emotions. There is a very low effect once income reaches $160,000 per year while $200,000 has no effect on reducing negative emotions.[20]

Giving away money can also make you feel happier. Brady Josephson suggests giving away small amounts of money frequently because it increases the pleasure high you feel when giving. The more frequently you give, the more you get to experience that good feeling. He discusses how the part of the brain that is responsible for pleasure and rewards, which is known as the amygdala, generates activity when we give. Brady mentioned that giving $1,000 all at one time doesn't give you ten times the high of giving $100 ten times.[21]

The important lesson we can take away from this is that we understand how to effectively use money and monitor our spending habits to help ensure we are using it in a way to ultimately bring us happiness. Remember that receiving money only makes us happy to a point, so we must obtain and use it wisely. Money is a tool to be used well and is not an end in itself. When we try to make it what it is not, we'll always feel empty.

THE BOTTOM LINE

- People are far more productive when they are engaged, excited, and fulfilled when they wake up in the morning.

- If you don't control your love of money, it will control you.

- Greed is the silent killer of happiness!

- The way to be happiest with money is not to look to it to provide happiness.

HAPPINESS NOW QUESTIONS

Destination: Where Do I Want to Go?

1. What are my long-term financial goals?

   _____

   _____

2. What type of financial cushion would I prefer to have in order to devote myself full-time to my dream career?

   _____

   _____

3. What would a reasonable financial increase look like for me over the next one, three, and five years?

   _____

   _____

4. What would it look like for me to achieve dreams and simultaneously feel secure financially?

   _____

   _____

5. How can I start giving towards causes and organizations that matter to me in the future? How much would I like to give away in my lifetime?

_____

_____

Location: Where Am I Now?

1. Do I feel competent to create financial stability and future financial success? Do I know how to create a budget or do I need to seek help?

_____

_____

2. What do I feel I am currently missing to feel secure financially?

_____

_____

3. What are my greatest financial needs?

_____

_____

4. How would I describe my current financial state, i.e. exceptional, above average, average, or below average? Why?

_____

_____

5. How much am I giving away now? Is this satisfactory? If not, what barriers are in my way?

_____

_____

Realization: What Do I Need to Change to Close the Gap?

1. What tools do I lack that will help me reach my financial goals? Do I need to enlist in a budgeting class, cut up some credit cards while I'm deep in debt, etc.?

_____

_____

2. What are my bottom-line financial needs currently?

_____

_____

3. What single word describes how I currently FEEL about where I am financially?

    _____

    _____

4. How do I allow my emotions to impact my spending, saving, and giving patterns?

    _____

    _____

5. What things do I NOT have control over that could negatively impact my financial position?

    _____

    _____

Acceleration: How Can I Best Move Forward Consistently?

1. What things do I have control over that upon making adjustments could alter my financial position?

    _____

    _____

2. What are some things I can do immediately to alter my current financial position for good?

_____

_____

3. Do I have access to people, resources, and professional/ trustworthy advice to support me in positioning myself for where I want to be long-term financially?

_____

_____

4. Do I have a financial "hero" who lives out the patterns of behavior and money mindset that I'd like to have in the future?

_____

_____

COORDINATE 2: FAMILY—INNER CIRCLE RELATIONSHIPS

"We are born in relationship, we are wounded in relationship, and we can be healed in relationship."

—Harville Hendrix

· ·

BIG IDEA
How healthy is your
family right now?

· ·

At first glance, it may seem odd that the second happiness coordinate for finding fulfillment in work and life has nothing to do with work—at least not directly. The reality is that, although we often say we keep work and family life separate, we all bring our work home with us at times—mentally and physically—and we bring family to work with us. If we're struggling at home, our work tends to suffer; if we're thriving at home, our work tends to benefit from those good relationships. Consequently, we suggest that inner circle relationships of family are critical to finding sustainable fulfillment.

Research by Bensinger, DuPont & Associates found that 47% of employees admitted their performance at work is affected by problems they are facing in their personal lives.[22] A study on performance interviewed 4,000 adults. The results showed that 15% of participants experienced a decrease in their productivity at work due to a separation or divorce.[23] According to the U.S. Department of Labor's Bureau of Labor Statistics, there has been a significant shift in marital and divorce rates in the last half century in our country.[24] Not surprisingly, disengagement and lack of fulfillment at work has increased accordingly. People are unhappy at home and unhappy at work. We believe the two are connected. Fewer people have happy family relationships to give them perspective and joy outside the workplace. Culture, media, propaganda, movies, and pornography are influencing marital relationships in our society—and usually not for the better. It's become normal for people to have hook ups, one-night stands, and affairs.

'THE TOUCHSTONE FOR FAMILY LIFE
IS STILL THE LEGENDARY 'AND SO THEY
WERE MARRIED AND LIVED HAPPILY EVER
AFTER.' IT IS NO WONDER THAT ANY FAMILY
FALLS SHORT OF THIS IDEA.'

SALVADOR MINUCHIN

As a result, emerging generations are questioning the foundation and essence of marriage all together. We both frequently speak with young people who hesitate to engage in marriage because of the many marital disasters they've seen. So many people have either been divorced, directly affected by divorce, or know someone else that has been negatively affected by it. The trauma that often comes from the pain of divorce has moved many people to run from it, especially Millennials.

Researcher, Meg Murphy, in a study on the delay of marriage, found that an unprecedented number of Millennials will remain unmarried until age forty. Marriage rates among Boomers came in at 91%, Late Boomers 87%, and Gen Xers 82%. The marriage rate among Millennials is expected to be around 70%, a substantial reduction.[25] Clearly, Millennials see marriage differently than previous generations. What's mind blowing to us is that so many are experiencing severe emotional discomfort as a result of being unwilling to commit—yet they remain unwilling to commit. The pain of staying the same has yet to exceed the pain of change. So they sit on the fence of the pain paradox.

DIFFICULTIES IN RELATIONSHIPS

Committed family relationships and healthy marriages are not easy. In fact, marriage is hard, even in the most ideal circumstances. Marital relationships provoke pain at times simply due to different life experiences, personal desires, and unmet expectations. When we don't feel our needs are being met—whether at home or at work—we experience pain, great or small. It eats away at us and, if left unchecked, will play out in our inner circle relationships. The levels of pain will vary when we face disappointment, depending upon our emotional, mental, and psychological states. Those of us who didn't have healthy relationships and marriages modeled for us will tend to struggle more.

The intensity of pain could be related to being raised by a single parent and not having the privilege of seeing a married couple resolve conflict in a healthy way. Others may have been raised by foster parents and, as a result, still experience the subconscious pain of abandonment. Even though they have every intention of not seeing their spouses or other family members through this lens, at times the trauma of childhood can overwhelm and resurface. You have your own story. Part of your story could include rape, verbal assaults, abortion, domestic violence, emotional abuse, neglect, or any number of factors that influence how you engage your family relationships or marriage.

Trauma has a way of changing how we see ourselves, our situations, and others because it actually changes us on a neurological level. Our brains are fascinating machines that not only help us make decisions on a day-to-day basis but also protect us from harm and alert us to potential danger. Trauma impacts various parts of the brain, including the prefrontal cortex (where we make decisions and solve complex problems), anterior cingulate cortex (where we are able to manage our emotions instead of being overwhelmed and overreacting when facing challenging situations), and the amygdala (where we detect information and discern if we need to be afraid and thus respond).

For example, if someone experienced trauma, his or her amygdala can become hyperactive and thus cause them to be easily stressed and have a hard time calming down after getting upset. The hyperactive amygdala can wreak havoc in a relationship where the husband has survived trauma but isn't aware of its impact. He may feel like his wife is attacking him when she points out that he forgot to take out the trash one day. If the husband came from an emotionally and verbally abusive home where his parents would berate him for not being perfect at household tasks, he might be on high alert whenever he feels anything close to those moments when he was yelled at by both parents.

The wife was simply pointing something out—something she thought was innocuous—but his hyperactive amygdala interpreted her neutral statement as an indictment, thus causing him to become defensive and lash out. As he lashes out, she becomes defensive and lashes out, as well. In only a few moments, what was a simple statement becomes the source of a weeklong fight between the couple. The husband is responsible for his words and actions, but the trauma impacted him on a subconscious level. Consequently, he can't differentiate, in the moment, whether something is a true threat or not. Those who have experienced trauma benefit from psychotherapy because it helps them process through the trauma and actually heal the way the brain responds to situations in the future.

Even if you haven't been through trauma, you've experienced dysfunction in relationships, probably in your family and in your early years. These dysfunctional patterns also impact how we relate as adults when we enter friendships, dating, and marriages. If someone grows up with a very critical and over protective parent, he or she is more likely to be critical of his or herself and become perfectionistic. This pattern can cause the person to become a pleaser in relationships, thinking that being perfect will cause the spouse to be happy and thus not criticize or critique. A child whose parents aren't emotionally supportive or physically present might become avoidant in relationships. Since the individual never learned how to have vulnerable, intimate relationships, he or she will repel people when they try to come close because it is so foreign and often uncomfortable.

WHILE FAMILY CAN DO A GREAT DEAL OF GOOD, WE ARE ALL SHAPED BY THOSE WHO LEFT A RELATIONAL IMPRINT ON US, FOR BETTER OR WORSE

To learn more about your relationship style, check out howwelove.com for a free quiz and helpful resources to help you discover your attachment style and discover ways to become the healthiest you can be in relationships.

ANTHONY'S OUTLOOK

My story and perspectives typify the family challenges so many must overcome and offers hope for finding sustainable happiness at home. While I learned a lot of positive things from the relationship between my mother and stepfather, I also spent a lot of years recovering from much of the dysfunction I saw in marriages, including theirs, as a child. I have invested hundreds of hours and thousands of dollars in marriage therapy, personal therapy, and executive coaching in order for my wife and I to have a thriving marriage. And, we still both agree that it's still a work in progress. I have read numerous books, listened to sermons and podcasts, and attended seminars.

Over the course of my own sixteen years of marriage (at the time of writing this book), I've learned what healthy marriages look like. Yet, in full transparency, I'm still working through some of the barriers of my childhood. My wife will be the first to say I don't always hit the target! I'm in a substantially healthier place today than I was many years ago, but I still have a long way to go.

As a black man in America, I'm even more concerned about the woeful marriage stats among minority groups. I can personally attest to the unhealthy state of marriages in the African American context. According to the Washing

Examiner, as many as 77% of black children in 2017 were born to single mothers. That is appalling, yet it speaks to the reality of the breakdown of the nuclear family in black culture.

A lot of influences impact these numbers, such as generational poverty, educational inequities, lack of transferrable career skills, and more. Although I'm certainly not making excuses for these influences, I do believe each of us who has experienced some success in family relationships has a responsibility to "reach back" and help others. In fact, for both Emily and me, we would not be able to help others now if it were not for family models and mentors who "reached back" to give us a vision beyond our own home environments.

If you are married and reading this book, the odds are that you are in a better position to help someone than most. Even if you are not in the ideal place you want to be in your marriage and family, and even though you might feel you have a lot to learn, you still have something to offer others. I once heard leadership speaker Andy Stanley say, "Do for one what you wish you could do for everyone!" If marriage and the strong foundation of family are to be restored, we must all be willing to invest in it. Let's shout from the mountaintops that marriage is still a great foundation.

Though not always easy, relational connection is definitely one of the keys to a fulfilling life. As Emily will attest, you can certainly be single and have strong relationships that cover you in hard times, but I would argue, and she would agree, that there is nothing like the fulfillment of two people walking together in the covenant of marriage.

ANTHONY'S OUTLOOK: PARENTING

Due to the pain of my own childhood, the hope of being a parent meant an opportunity to script a different story. On September 15th, 2002, I embraced the challenge as I held my son. I remember holding my son in my arms for the first time and weeping incessantly, overwhelmed with joy. I was committed to being a praying, faithful, loving, present, and emotionally engaging father—a father who would literally take a bullet for his kid. I got to experience that joy all over again in October 2005 when God blessed me with the most beautiful baby girl on the planet.

While the joys and challenges of parenthood have been equally overwhelming at times, I cannot imagine a more powerful motivation than knowing that every single morning I rise, there are two dependent souls counting on me to love them unconditionally. I count it a privilege to pray, provide, push, punish when necessary, and prepare them for living a purposeful life. I consider fatherhood one of the greatest privileges a man could ever have in life. Yet, parenting has its challenges as well. In the world where I came from, there are tens of thousands of dead-beat dads (and moms) giving birth to children every day.

Believe me, I've heard every excuse imaginable as to why fathers and mothers forsake their children. Both Emily and I understand the excuses and know that family struggles are not restricted to those living in poverty. An article in *Psychology Today* showed that the offspring from affluent parents are often *more* distressed than other youth.[26] Children of wealthy parents can have disturbingly high rates of substance use, depression, anxiety, eating disorders, cheating, and stealing. If parents with all of the resources in the world sometimes have great difficulties raising kids, can you imagine what it must be like for parents that come from backgrounds of severe poverty and broken families?

I'm not excusing their behaviors at all, but the bottom line is you cannot give what you do not possess. The deadbeats in the world are likely modeling the same behaviors they've seen modeled for them. In many cases, family failure is often all they've known. As Maya Angelou says, "You do the best you can until you know better. Then when you know better, you do better!"

Marriage and parenting are by far the most difficult things I have ever done. I did not necessarily have the greatest models. My mother and father were teenagers when I was born, and they never married. When my stepfather arrived, we could finally overcome poverty although we still lived in an apartment in the hood for my primary years. Even when we eventually bought a home in a lower, middle-class community, it was not fully furnished until after I graduated high school. I never felt like I was missing anything, however, as both my stepfather and mother worked hard to provide for the family.

Yet, our house was an emotional wreck. There was a constant emotional tug of war between them with constant tension. For example, when I was in fourth grade, I woke up one morning having wet the bed again during the night. Because I had been beaten by my stepfather previously for doing it, I had what I thought was a clever idea. I placed my pajama pants over an electric heater to dry and then began to make my bed. While stressing over whether my stepfather would find out, I burned a hole in the pants. Consequently, I balled the pants up inside my coat and, when I went out to play with my friends, I trashed them in the apartment community dumpster. No one ever found out.

The fact that I was wetting the bed as a fourth grader indicated the stress I—and a lot of my friends—experienced as part of our family lives. Consequently, when people question how I am able to cope with the stress of parenting today, I consider the positive stress a privilege compared to my negative childhood stress. I don't see it as a curse, but as a blessing. The massive downside to my life story is that I've had to learn about parenting the hard way. I've made so many mistakes by doing stupid things and repeating some of the destructive patterns I saw growing up. I've yelled at my son and daughter unnecessarily and placed unhealthy demands on them at times. But after engaging in therapy and reeducating myself, I've been able to break the cycle and now have an incredible relationship with my son and daughter. In fact, I tell them both that my long-term success is defined by having long-term, healthy relationships with both of them and their families. It's not just words for me. This really is my model for success. This version of success can't be bought. It has to be earned.

The bottom line is that money and career success can't replace a destructive relationship with a positive relationship. There is nothing more important on earth than having a phenomenal relationship with your family. Nothing. If you want to be happy, focus on your family, and the fulfillment you experience there will dramatically affect the fulfillment you enjoy at work.

ANTHONY'S OUTLOOK: MEMORIES

It brings me great joy to be writing these words at three in the morning after Christmas Day. My wife and kids are soundly asleep as I sit poolside, pounding away on my laptop while enjoying the temperate, early-morning weather in Orlando, Florida. We have had the best time over the last several days and the saddest part for me is that it has to come to an end soon. I don't live in a fantasyland. I really do look forward to getting back home and preparing to kick the new work year off with a bang. I love what I have the privilege of doing for a living and am not complaining at all. Having the opportunity to inspire others through my work is exceptionally fulfilling. Yet, nothing matters more to me than the opportunity to share unforgettable experiences and memories with my family. There's simply nothing like it.

For almost three quarters of my life, I did not experience such joy. It was not modeled well for me, partly because it was not modeled for my stepfather or mother either. We lacked an appreciation for unique family experiences outside the routine and we didn't have discretionary income to spend on vacations. Even if we had, I am not convinced the mood in our household would have made family vacations all that enjoyable. As I grew and developed some sense of independence, I spent a substantial amount of time away from home, hanging out at the community parks and the homes of friends where we would play basketball, tackle football, ride bikes, or play imaginative games, because we didn't have high-tech gadgets.

One such game was "that's my car." Because families in the hood couldn't afford the nicest vehicles, we would sit on the curbs of busy streets and look for nice vehicles to pass by and yell, "That's my car!" when we saw one we hoped to have one day. The one who yelled quickest and the loudest would "win the car." There wasn't a lot of family fun available to us, so we had to create our own.

My outlook changed when I was bussed to Germantown (a predominantly white, higher-income community) for middle school. It changed the way I thought about families doing life, vacations, and creating memories together. I made a personal commitment to create a similar reality for my own family with a legacy of unforgettable memories.

But it has not been an easy thing to do. My extended family and friends from childhood have struggled to understand why we would want to create family memories and unique experiences the way we choose to do. As Will Smith stated in his song, "Parents Just Don't Understand, " those who grew up in the hood have a hard time because their worldview is so exceptionally limited.[27] I get it. Accepting cultural norms outside of my own was extremely difficult for me initially.

For example, I was twelve when I first had the opportunity to have a memorable interaction with a white kid. I had never really been outside of my own neighborhood context, so the thought of embracing other cultural norms was something I couldn't even fathom. Even in our tech-connected age with easy transportation, the same is true of a lot of kids today. Their memories are limited to the world they live in every day.

Many people are shocked by this notion, but think about it—how does the cycle stop without exposure to other options? My maternal great grandparents, for example, lived in a three-room shack in rural Southaven, MS. The bathroom was an outhouse, the running water was outside in the grass, and anyone who wanted access had to step on wooden pallets to get to either. My great grandfather couldn't read, and my great grandmother never went past a first-grade education. They were sharecroppers who eventually inherited land. My maternal grandmother had five nervous breakdowns throughout her life, never learned to drive, never rented a property of her own—let alone owned anything—and died in her early 60s. My mother was left to fend for herself for the most part. Although she radically improved the circumstances of her life, she still became a teenage mother and struggled to overcome her own limitations as well.

Consequently, I will continue to be intentional about creating memories with my family, exploring new places, and broadening their experiences to create a new family *normal* for our own nuclear family. We plan to continue to travel both domestically and internationally to see parts of the world I never would have imagined seeing while growing up. As we continue to mature in this area of family, I'm experiencing joy beyond my wildest expectations—a joy unthinkable in my childhood years. Now as I continue to peel back the layers of pain, I will not allow anything to take precedence over bringing our family together for extended periods to create everlasting memories.

I know the joy I'll experience on my deathbed will be directly related to how well I create memories with my family. It will have nothing to do with what I drove, where I lived, or the assets I accumulated. Instead, my fulfillment then will depend on how well I turn minutes into moments and moments into memories.

THE BOTTOM LINE

- Though not always easy, relational connection is one of the keys to a fulfilling life.
- Money and career success can't replace the pain that needs to heal from a destructive relationship.
- Do your own work first before looking to others.
- If you focus on your family, the fulfillment you experience there will dramatically affect the fulfillment you enjoy at work.
- While family can do a great deal of good, we are all shaped by those who left a relational imprint on us, for better or worse.

HAPPINESS NOW QUESTIONS

Destination: Where Do I Want to Go?

1. What does family mean to me exactly?

    _____

    _____

2. How do I want my own family to be when compared to
    my family of origin (the family with whom I grew up)?

    _____

    _____

3. What legacy do I want to leave with my family? What's
    the highest compliment my spouse and kids can say
    about me at my funeral?

    _____

    _____

4. What vision do I have for my family long-term?

    _____

    _____

5. How would I define "success" for my family?

_____

_____

6. What role do I desire my family to play in my long-term perspective on happiness?

_____

_____

Location: Where am I Now?

1. How would I define the current state of my family? Is it healthy or unhealthy? Why?

_____

_____

2. What is the greatest challenge I see facing my family today?

_____

_____

3. What are the current barriers, if any, preventing my family from being as happy and whole as I desire?

    _____

    _____

Realization: What do I Need to Change to Close the Gap?

1. What role am I currently playing in impacting the areas of growth for my family?

    _____

    _____

2. What about my current lifestyle or behavioral paradigm highly influences the current state of my nuclear and extended family?

    _____

    _____

3. What two or three relationships in my close circle of family and friends have brought me the most pain? How? Why?

    _____

    _____

4. Healed wounds don't leak. Sometimes, we think that we have healed, but when someone bumps up against a past pain, we leak infectious words and reactions. In my life, what are the areas of past pain, trauma, or hurtful relationships in my family of origin that I need to process through, forgive, and heal from?

_____

_____

5. What people can I include in this process to offer guidance and accountability? (Please note that we are not encouraging you to enter back into relationships with toxic and abusive people. You can process through old pain and forgive your offenders, even if they aren't present. Be sure to enlist the help of a trained professional to help you navigate through past pain and trauma so it leads you to greater healing and not cause additional trauma.)

_____

_____

Acceleration: How Can I Best Move Forward Consistently?

1. What can I immediately change about myself that would ultimately impact my current family structure for good?

    _____

    _____

2. Although I cannot fully own others' happiness, what can I do to positively influence the happiness of my immediate family members or friends?

    _____

    _____

3. What three things will I consistently do in the next 90 days to alter the trajectory of my family's happiness?

    _____

    _____

COORDINATE 3: COMMUNITY—OUTER CIRCLE RELATIONSHIPS

"When we honestly ask ourselves which persons in our lives mean the most to us, we often find that it is those who, instead of giving advice, solutions, or cures, have chosen rather to share our pain and touch our wounds with a warm and tender hand. The friend who can be silent with us in a moment of despair or confusion, who can stay with us in an hour of grief and bereavement, who can tolerate not knowing, not curing, not healing and face with us the reality of our powerlessness, that is a friend who cares."

—Henri Nouwen

. . . .

BIG IDEA
How healthy are your friendships?

. . . .

Getting clear on your Family coordinate, or inner-circle relationships, is critical, but other outer-circle relationships can affect your happiness, too. The Gallup Well-Being Index affirms that people who experience more fulfilled lives have relationships outside of immediate family that keep them balanced and happy. Friendships, co-workers, romantic relationships, and fellow students—anyone with whom you connect on a regular basis forms your community. The people you surround yourself with on a regular basis impact your growth and the direction of your life, and vice versa. Who you choose to place in your community, and how you choose to influence your community, will directly influence your potential for happiness.

> 'IN A FUTILE ATTEMPT TO ERASE OUR PAST, WE DEPRIVE THE COMMUNITY OF OUR HEALING GIFT. IF WE CONCEAL OUR WOUNDS OUT OF FEAR AND SHAME, OUR INNER DARKNESS CAN NEITHER BE ILLUMINATED NOR BECOME A LIGHT FOR OTHERS.'
>
> BRENNAN MANNING

We came from very different communities growing up, yet we both had our fair share of positive and negative experiences. Anthony shared earlier about how growing up in the hood shaped his life and worldview. Emily also knows firsthand just how much a community can negatively affect your happiness if you let it. Community can be healthy and positive or it can be degrading and negative.

EMILY'S OUTLOOK: YOU ARE ENOUGH

When I was young, my life was rather homogenous. During school, we all learned the same things, went from one class to another—all in a straight line, and worked together so that our class won as many games as we could at the end-of-year field day. We were all smart and talented in our own ways, but as we grew older the differences became more pronounced. My goal was to fit in like everyone else. Anything that made me look different became a source of self-loathing.

I didn't realize I was doing it at the time, but I didn't want parts of me displayed on my parents' fridge. For example, I would wear bows twice the size of my head with big, thick pink glasses covering half my face on picture day to distract from my appearance. It got to me when my dance teacher told me I was not measuring up to my classmates because I was "fat" and didn't look like them. If I wanted to succeed, she said, I needed to lose weight. I was only ten when she grabbed my stomach and told me that I needed to lose the fat. My heart broke. I wasn't enough. I've struggled with that message off and on ever since. My story is probably similar to some part of your own story because we've all been told that we aren't enough in some way or another.

Most children feel like they are enough until they're told something different. When most people see a baby, they instantly *ooh* and *aah*. They don't critique the baby, point out flaws, or complain how he or she isn't contributing to the national GDP. Nope. The baby is precious and adored simply because it exists. But somewhere after infancy, we got the message that we have to do or be something in order to be acceptable, worthy, valued, and enough. Not only are we told we don't measure up, we also start measuring ourselves to others.

Toddlers don't play the comparison game. They don't compare intellect, begrudge sports skills, or covet their classmate's thigh gap. They don't know or care what those things are in the first place. They only think about snack time, playing, and finding ways to get out of nap times. As I work with teens and young adults, I hear common concerns that, at the core, are based on the fears of not being enough. I ask them where they first received this message, not to condemn someone else, but to explain, heal, and move forward.

Think about this in your own life. Where did you first learn to compare? When were you told that you didn't measure up? I encourage you to look at those places in your life and give yourself space to process the experience so you can exchange those false beliefs with truth. Let that truth be the anthem you shout over and above the old and unhelpful lies spoken to you by a critical dance teacher, a distant parent, or a broken society.

On your own or with the help of a trusted therapist, write out truths about yourself. Give yourself a healthy dose of new self-talk by reading them several times a day for the next month. It will literally retrain how your brain works and how you see yourself. You cannot erase old messages, but you can surround yourself with reminders of the truth—you are more than enough.

Enough doesn't mean you are perfect. You have value because you are a human being, not because you are a human *doing*. Your value doesn't depend on how much you can produce and how much you do to please others. Know that you are worthy, you are loved, and you are valuable no matter what anyone else may or may not say.

EMILY'S OUTLOOK: WORTHY OF LOVE AND BELONGING

Just like job titles, your relationship status shouldn't define your worth, although it often does, unfortunately. Whether you are single, dating, married, divorced, or widowed, it's easy to compare your path to others and, even worse, the path you previously planned in your own head. This problematic pattern of comparison causes individuals to constantly look ahead for the next relationship step instead of being content with growth in their current state.

Far too many singles come into my office wishing they were dating. Then when they find someone, they anxiously try to determine if he or she is "the one." The mental sprint from first date to monogrammed towels and wedding dresses happens at lightning-fast speed for some people, often without the other person in the relationship knowing about it.

Beth was a perfect example. She met Brad while they were both in their mid 20s. From the first date, Beth was smitten by Brad and painted him into the perfect dream of their future together. Consequently, Beth had a hard time seeing the fundamental differences between her and Brad, because she was already ten steps ahead, planning their future life together. She was filled with an aching sense of loneliness that she believed would only be filled by a relationship like the one she envisioned.

Watching wedding TV shows and being a bridesmaid in ten of her friend's weddings only reinforced her obsession. Going to a wedding as a single person often left her feeling like she was less than her peers who had partners. But with Brad now in the picture, this feeling of not being enough went away. It wasn't until Brad abruptly broke up with her a year later that she realized her dreams with Brad would never become a reality. She had fallen in love with the idea of Brad, but not Brad himself.

Beth's premature acceleration of the relationship robbed her of learning more about him, listening to her own reservations, and taking counsel from friends to slow the process down. Her situation serves as a powerful reminder not to force relationships and not to measure the value of relationships by a life plan that doesn't include the other person.

As a counselor, I have often seen that, for the most part, women's greatest insecurities are relational, while men's greatest insecurities are occupational. Women primarily express fears of not being enough in counseling, so if you are a woman who related to Beth's story, know you are not alone. Ever since childhood, women watch movies and read books with characters in search of "true love" to save the princesses and other damsels in distress. As someone who has been single for many years, I know better than most that such tales can leave you feeling insufficient. Holidays like Valentine's Day only heighten that feeling amongst single women, especially single professional women who struggle to feel accepted in the workplace based on their accomplishments.

EMILY'S OUTLOOK:
SINGLES, YOU ARE ENOUGH

It's easy to forget you are enough when everything around you is telling you that you are only half a person. It's amazing how I can have a doctorate degree, run a successful business, have a healthy family and friendships, serve in my community and on various oversees mission trips, yet some people bypass all the wonderful things in my life and only focus on my being single.

Questions like, "Why are you still single?" or "What's wrong that you aren't married yet?" don't feel like questions. They feel more like judgments and accusations implying that something is wrong. In reality, they are reflections of the person asking and what he or she values most. Thankfully, those comments don't bother me anymore, but I know they can be troubling to some, especially when relationship struggles touch a place of deep insecurity. Often, as a single person, it can feel like you're left in life's waiting room while everyone else gets called for his or her appointments with destiny. While everyone else is enjoying a fairytale relationship, you're left with a pile of old magazines and elevator music. No, thank you!

"You complete me." Not only is this a cheesy phrase popularized by the movie *Jerry McGuire*, it's also false.

The oft-quoted expression places an inappropriate and impossible expectation onto the other person in the relationship. Relationships certainly make life more vibrant, but they don't complete you and make you a whole person. Relationships and partners don't fill in the spaces where you've been hurt by a parent, for example, nor do they fill the voids you have from past pain. They can add color but not fulfill every life dream, goal, and purpose.

If you look to relationships to define who you are and give you purpose in life, you'll be left discouraged and resentful when your expectations aren't met. Our relationships are only as healthy as the people in them—and one of those people will always be *you*. So let's start there.

BEING HAPPY WITH YOURSELF AND YOUR LIFE IS YOUR RESPONSIBILITY

If you look for other people to make you happy, you'll only feel deeply disappointed when you never receive what you were lacking in the first place. The man unhappy with his job will still be unhappy with his job regardless of his relationships. The woman struggling with a low self-esteem will still have a low self-esteem regardless of her relationships. In fact, the relationship will probably only magnify the low self-esteem! Relationships only provide opportunities to reveal who you are; they don't magically solve everything. They only accentuate what's already present in the lives of both people.

Several decades of research have equipped Dr. John Gottman to predict with 94% certainty whether a couple will break up, stay together and be unhappy, or stay together as a happy couple[28]. His predictions apply across the board— straight, gay, rich, poor, and in homes with and without children. Gottman found that the best predictors of success and happiness in relationships are whether or not people bring kindness and generosity to a relationship instead of contempt, constant criticism, and hostility.[29]

If you are single, you have the opportunity to work on yourself so you can bring the healthiest version of you to the relationship. You can learn how to be quick to listen, forgive, and make amends so you can do it well in your future relationships.

FRIENDSHIPS

Friendships are a lot like teams, providing a place of being and belonging. Friendships are not limited to a certain age, marital status, career, culture, or socioeconomic class. Family is given to us, but the benefits of friendship can be even more pronounced because those relationships are intentional. A large body of evidence supports the reality that friendships increase mood, physical, and psychological health. One study even found that friendship was the most important factor that determined one's happiness, contributing to the satisfaction of other areas of life like health, personal achievement, and overall satisfaction.[30]

Ed Diener and Martin Seligman, two pioneers of the positive psychology movement, conducted a 2002 study that revealed the common components amongst the happiest students.[31] The top 10% reported having strong friendships and spending time with those friends.[32] Fulfilling the desire to belong is not optional, but necessary for those who want to be truly happy.

What do friends offer? Everything! They impact our health, mental wellness, and career success. For example, college students who have strong friendships were found to be half as likely to catch a cold.[33] Their resilience to physical illness is higher because friends offer the additional support necessary when fighting diseases and lowering risk factors. Another study showed that friendships are as beneficial as quitting smoking, regular exercise, and maintaining a healthy weight.[34] Those who start an exercise plan are more likely to keep and continue it more than a year later when social support is present.

Friendships can even impact when you die. Based upon a review of over 140 studies, people with strong friendships are 50% less likely to die prematurely.[35] Our memories and intellectual faculties worsen as we age, but people without close friendships experience memory decline two times faster than those who are socially integrated.

Friendships are essential to our mental health.

OUR PERSPECTIVES BECOME FAR MORE
OPTIMISTIC WHEN WE HAVE DAILY SOURCES
OF SOCIAL SUPPORT.

Though the stressors might still exist, the perception of challenges changes. We see them as more doable and recover from stressful situations faster when reminded of friendships. Friendships significantly decrease the risk of suicide, anxiety, and depression. Women are more likely to reach out and express their stress to friends. However, when men reach out to friends, they tend to live longer and have more satisfying relationships overall. Friends help make challenges seem less daunting and those reaching out to friends during stressful seasons produce less of the stress hormone cortisol.

Friendships impact career productivity, because workplace friends make employees feel more satisfied with their work, inspire greater motivation, and increase job satisfaction.[36] Friends can make you feel richer, too! According to the National Bureau of Economic Research, doubling your group of friends has the same effect on your happiness as getting a 50% raise.[37]

All things are not created equal, and the same is true for friendships. Regardless of the quantity of Facebook friends and social media followers, we encourage you to look for quality. Friendships that are face-to-face have more benefits than those found solely on social media sites. In one study, the correlation reported from online friendship and happiness was zero in most cases and even negative in some cases.[38] Why? When conversations are limited to a small amount of characters or likes, connections also remain limited. Thus you can have hundreds or even thousands of friends and followers on social media, but would only vacation with, go to the weddings of, and share your struggles with a handful of them.

Emily has seen real friendships be particularly helpful for those who are going through significant life challenges and difficulties like the death of a parent, a cancer diagnosis, or a divorce. Calling all the friends into her office, she has watched them surround the hurting client and link arms in the days and weeks to follow. Asking for help is human. We all need to do it from time to time. And when we know those friendships will be there for us, we're better positioned to find our way through the pain.

No one can do it alone. If you find yourself or a friend in a similarly hard time, we encourage you to find your tribe— your circle of trusted friends whose love speaks louder than the darkness, pain, and self-doubt. Let these precious souls into the painful parts of your life so you can get through to the other side and serve them in the same way.

CASE STUDY: COLLEAGUES AND MENTORS

Ana was a medical school student struggling with severe anxiety. Ana's father and mother loved her but put a lot of pressure on her to become a physician. First-generation immigrants themselves, they wanted to instill a strong work ethic in her and help her pursue her dreams by pushing her to perform academically. Regardless of her scores, her father would always critique her report cards class by class, investigating ways she could improve or helping her make higher scores next time. She adopted her parents' high standards as her own, but lacked the coping skills to manage the high-stress level and hard workload.

Then she met Karen, a physician and mentor to first-year medical students. Karen knew the pressures of medical school and experienced the benefits of having a mentor when she was struggling. Karen invited Ana to come to her office after classes to study and spent time reviewing test questions so she'd be best prepared for her medical boards. She invited Ana to medical seminars and networking functions to remind Ana of what she was working towards. Karen knew it was critical to have someone walk with Ana through the interview process for future residencies and fellowships in their competitive field of medicine. On her own, Ana was on her way to crumbling under the pressures. With helpful guidance from her mentor, however, she was able to become successful beyond her own high expectations.

Just like Ana, we all benefit from having mentors. Research shows that high-quality mentoring relationships have a powerful impact on mentees in personal, professional, and academic situations.[39] Through the mentoring relationship, mentees are able to learn how to improve skills and receive feedback in a less intimidating manner, as it would be with a boss or manager. Learning from someone else's mistakes allows the mentee to avoid negative outcomes and costly mistakes.

Both of us have been on both the giving and receiving end of mentoring relationships. We've seen how having a veteran walk side by side with a younger, less experienced professional is indispensable to growth and success. Such a relationship provides a practical classroom where questions are welcome and it's okay to admit you don't know everything. The relationship also benefits the mentor, as he or she is able to see impact on future generations in the workforce, family, or other areas of life.

EMILY'S OUTLOOK: MENTORING

I found mentoring to be incredibly helpful to me when I started my practice in the middle of the largest recession since the Great Depression! When other businesses were closing, I was starting from scratch with no financial backing and without having ever taken a business class in college. Regardless of how many degrees I had, I knew I had a lot to learn about starting and running a business. The more I learned, the more I realized how much I didn't know. When I was told that building a practice typically takes three years, I quickly surrounded myself with people far more savvy and experienced than I was and created a full patient load within nine months! From *New York Times* bestselling authors to seasoned therapists, I absorbed everything like a sponge when in their presence. I'm quite sure I must have been the dumbest person in the room, but I wanted to sit at the feet of brilliant businesspeople. Life was in session, and I made sure I had the best professors possible!

These people served as my personal board of directors, handpicked for their specific skills and insights. Before making any significant moves, I looked to them for advice. Usually they had words of wisdom, insights, and even guidance for what *not* to do based upon their own experience. They learned their lessons the hard way and helped me not waste valuable time or money making similar mistakes. Sometimes their feedback was painful and humbling, like when I had gone to great lengths with a specific marketing campaign, business plan, or potential new hire.

A few times when I had already started down a path and poured a lot of time and money into something, they strongly encouraged me to reconsider. Sometimes I would push back initially, but ultimately I realized that they were trying to protect me from making some really stupid decisions. Being transparent about my goals and holding my goals loosely as I engaged with my "board of directors" was uncomfortable at times, but I became wiser faster because of it.

ANTHONY'S OUTLOOK: MENTORING

Mentoring has been incredibly helpful for me also. I am more than convinced there is no way I would be where I am today without the support and belief of people in my life who resembled the direction I wanted to go long term.

I knew when I was younger that I wanted to grow up, graduate from college, get married, have children, be a businessman, and impact the world around me. The problem was I had no idea exactly how all of that would come to pass. I am grateful other people saw enough in me—things I often did not see myself—to be willing to take the time and invest the energy for me to grow to the next level.

Today, I have several mature adults in my life who I consider to be mentors. Although most of them consider themselves to be "friends," I have so much value and respect for who they are and the impact they have had on my life that I cannot help but see parts of who they are as "mentorship arenas." I glean incredible value from them that has heavily impacted the overall trajectory of my life. Simply put, I would not be the husband, father, man of faith, businessman, or community leader I have become without the voice and influence of so many others over the years.

While it sounds cliché, I really do stand on the shoulders of giants and highly encourage anyone who does not have mentors in their lives to change that immediately. You need them. No one is self-made. We all have benefited from the labor, sweat equity, and price paid by someone else at one point or another.

LIVING IN COMMUNITY

We believe life is better lived within and surrounded by community—not riding solo. We encourage you to find seasoned, wise mentors to offer counsel on your career journey. Mark Batterson, an innovative leader and communicator, suggests having mentors because we all have blind spots and need to give people permission to speak the truth in love.[40] Wise advisors will say what we need to hear, not what we want to hear.

Being mentored will empower you to grow faster so you can, in turn, mentor others. Even if you aren't a CEO or C-suite executive, you have an opportunity to lead others. As John C. Maxwell says, "Everyone is a leader, because everyone influences someone…. The bottom line in leadership isn't how far we advance ourselves but how far we advance others. That is achieved by serving others and adding value to their lives."

We believe true happiness in our work is directly related to your ability to be influenced by and to influence others, to work together to cultivate change and progress. Consider whom you might intentionally influence in your life, through work, church or civic organization. Wherever it may be, we know that it will be time and effort that have a significant

ROI. In the words of Jackie Robinson, "A life isn't significant except for its impact on other lives."

THE BOTTOM LINE

- If you look to relationships to define who you are and give you purpose in life, you'll be left discouraged and resentful when your expectations aren't met.
- Relationships only provide opportunities to reveal who you are; they don't magically solve everything. They accentuate what's already present in the lives of both people.
- Satisfaction is directly related to having a strong circle of influencers and those you are influencing. We thrive better together.
- The people you surround yourself with on a regular basis impact your growth and the direction of your life.

HAPPINESS NOW QUESTIONS

Destination: Where Do I Want to Go?

1. Three "reach" candidates for mentorship in my life in the next five years are _____, _____, and _____.

2. Three candidates I can immediately access for mentorship in my life in the next year are _____, _____, and _____.

3. What do I want to see change relative to my outer-circle community of relationships in the next three to five years?

    _____

    _____

4. What would an ideal mentoring relationship look like for me?

    _____

    _____

5. What do I want my friendships to look like ten years from now?

    _____

    _____

Location: Where am I now?

1. What areas do I feel are strong as it pertains to my outer circle of community?

    _____

    _____

2. What are some things I consider to be absent in my life as it pertains to my outer circle of community?

    _____

    _____

3. Are there any areas of ambiguity in my life as it pertains to my outer circle of community? If so, what are the areas?

    _____

    _____

4. Are the friends in my life now going to help me become the person I aim to become in my personal life, in my relationships, and in my career? Are any of them holding me back from making progress?

_____

_____

Realization: What Do I Need to Change to Close the Gap?

1. What three things would I like to fix immediately in order to positively alter my outer circle of community?

_____

_____

2. What are three things I can immediately implement pertaining to my outer circle of community?

_____

_____

Acceleration: How Can I Best Move Forward Consistently?

1. In life, we have several tiers of friends. The closest tier is composed of people in your "inner circle" they are your safest people, those who are loyal, healthy,

and supportive of you. The second tier are friends and acquaintances, those you would invite to social events and grab dinner together, but not share your most private information and vulnerabilities with. The third tier makes up acquaintances and those in your community like parents on the PTA, people at church, and your neighbors.

2. Take a moment and write out who belongs in each tier and then look at how much time you spend with each tier. Often, we see people pouring their already-limited free time and energy into tier two and three relationships when tier one relationships are the healthiest and most life-giving. We challenge you to change that a bit by spending the majority of your free time with tier one people and offering the extra time to tiers two and then three. Try this out for sixty to ninety days and see how your satisfaction in relationships and in your life in general increases.

Tier One:

_____

Tier Two:

_____

Tier Three:

_____

3. Who can you invite to be on your board of personal
    directors? We encourage you to consider a handful of
    individuals and take them to coffee for a one-on-one
    meeting. Ask them if they would be willing to play this
    role in your life for twelve months and if they agree, be
    sure to touch base with them throughout the year when
    making critical life and career decisions. Bring them
    into the conversation and decision-making process and
    review any successes and failures you make along the
    way with their more objective and discerning eye. Feel
    free to keep them on the board for future years if it is a
    fit or invite others to rotate in if you feel like someone
    else might be a better fit, based upon life situations and
    changes.

_____

_____

COORDINATE 4: PHYSICAL—ENERGY AND SUSTAINABILITY

"Action may not always bring happiness, but there is no happiness without action."

—William James

· ·

BIG IDEA
Is your physical health a priority in your life?

· ·

YOUR PHYSICAL HEALTH DETERMINES YOUR ENERGY LEVELS AND YOUR CAPACITY TO SUSTAIN SUCCESS

That might be important to you if you want to be happy. In the day-to-day rush of getting things done, busy professionals can easily overlook the effect that physical health has on feeling fulfilled. When we feel depleted, we struggle to maintain a positive attitude and keep our focus in the other coordinates. When we optimize the physical coordinate, however, we empower and position ourselves to thrive in all coordinates.

Can you be happy without being physically healthy? Absolutely. In fact, some of the happiest people in the world are those who deal with physical limitations, illnesses, or diseases on a daily basis. But everyone can maximize the health capacity they have been given. Eating in a healthy way, exercising regularly, and getting adequate sleep, for example, can position you to stay true to your purpose in the face of work and life circumstances. Keeping healthy habits helps you stay on track with your finances and have the energy to engage relationships, both in your family and broader community. Sustainable energy is critical to following the Happiness Map you choose to pursue.

HAPPINESS AND YOUR HEALTH

The connection between happiness and health is more of a cycle than a question of *which came first: the chicken or the egg?* Healthy life habits unlock your potential for fulfillment in other areas. A physically healthy person will have the energy and stamina to take other coordinates to the next level and pursue his or her life purpose with greater passion. Research shows that people who regularly exercise are happier, and people who are happier also exercise regularly.[41]

However there's more to it than physical benefits. Healthy habits actually improve your brain health, which impacts your mental performance. Your brain health impacts your likelihood to succeed on tests, to be on your game for interviews, and to be creative and fully present at work. Thus, sweating in the gym translates into success in the boardroom.

Recent research from the University of Illinois at Urbana-Champaign shows that the brain's white matter—the network of nerve fibers that connect and transmit brain signals from one part of the brain to another—becomes more fibrous and compact with physical exercise. According to athlete and author Christopher Bergland, "the more streamlined and compact your white matter is, the faster and more efficiently your brain functions."[42] What this means is that regular physical exercise every day helps you retain and build your brain's white matter. A study from the department of psychology and neuroscience at Dartmouth found that people who had exercised for one month significantly improved their scores on memory and mood tests. The volunteers who had exercised for the past month, *and who exercised on the day of testing for results*, performed the best on the memory and mood exam, and had less anxiety.[43] Wouldn't that go a long way to making you happier today?

Most of us have a general idea of what happens to the body when we exercise. If we're training correctly, we build more muscle or stamina.

DAILY ACTIVITIES BECOME EASIER IF WE EXERCISE REGULARLY.

The stairs to the office don't leave us winded when used daily in lieu of elevators. We get that. However, the benefits of physical exercise to our brain and mood are a little harder to envision. We may know it has something to do with "endorphins being released," but what does that mean?

Here's what actually happens in simple terms. When you engage in physical exercise, your brain recognizes increased stress to your body. Your heart rate and blood pressure increase, producing hormones that begin your natural "fight or flight" response.[44] To protect from the stress, your body releases a protein called Brain-Derived Neurotrophic Factor (BDNF).[45] BDNF acts as a reset switch for your brain as it protects and repairs your memory neurons. That's why you often feel more at ease and have greater clarity after exercising. At the same time, endorphins release in your brain to fight the stress. Researcher M.K. McGovern reports that endorphins, "minimize the discomfort of exercise, block the feeling of pain, and are even associated with a feeling of euphoria."[46]

Bottom line: we turn on our brains when we exercise and feel better because of it. BDNF and endorphins makes us feel so good when we exercise. They can be quite addictive, not unlike morphine, heroine, or nicotine. The difference is that physical exercise is good for you—just don't let it control your life. Now, to be candid, most of us have the opposite problem—finding time to work exercise into our schedules. For all of us who don't want to live at the gym, there's good news.

To get the most benefits from exercise, you don't need to become a professional athlete, unless that aligns with your life purpose. In fact, it doesn't take much exercise to reach the peak benefits for happiness and productivity in everyday life. *New York Times* best-selling author Gretchen Reynolds says, "The first 20 minutes of moving around, if someone has been really sedentary, provide most of the health benefits. You get prolonged life, reduced disease risk—all of those things come in in the first 20 minutes of being active."[47]

Don't think we're saying you have to become a gym rat to feel fulfilled! All it takes is 20 minutes of focused, intense, and effective exercise every day to give yourself a healthy, happiness boost—especially on workdays. When people exercised on workdays, "their mood significantly improved after exercising. Mood stayed about the same on days they didn't, with the exception of people's sense of calm which deteriorated."[48] In other words, when you're working hard, exercise reduces the amount of stress you're feeling and frees you to focus on what matters most. Exercise also causes the production of a protein called PGC-1alpha, which has been shown to break down kynurenine, a stress-induced substance that accumulates in the bloodstream.[49] Thus, you can reduce your risk of becoming depressed and *stressed out* by exercising! Clearly, regular physical exercise does more than build muscle. It builds your brain and prepares you to perform at your best.

EMILY'S OUTLOOK:
THE POWER OF THE PHYSICAL

When working with clients, I find I can gauge their happiness levels more fully by discovering their sleep, eating, and exercise habits. In fact, those areas can help determine if someone is depressed. For some, depressive symptoms could be significantly reduced through regular physical exercise. If you can't exercise every day, exercising for thirty minutes three times a week is the equivalent of taking an antidepressant, but without any potentially negative side effects.[50] After all, what did people do before we started prescribing antidepressants? Yes, there is certainly a time and place for medication but it isn't a cure all for patients, especially those who aren't cultivating healthy lifestyle habits as part of the treatment plan. For many generations before us, people went outside, got Vitamin D from the sun, and stayed active. They went to sleep when it got dark and awoke with the dawn. Now we prescribe drugs that minimize symptoms without dealing with the actual problem. We're not saying people were never depressed before, but we're seeing depression reach epidemic proportions today even as our sedentary lifestyle increases.

It seems like we live in a microwave culture where we want to have instant happiness with little-to-no wait time, effort, and pain involved. We want fulfillment without effort and good results without doing the work. Most people want to take the easy way out, because they think they don't want to handle the difficulty or don't see how daily habits like exercising can actually benefit them. The irony is that the more work you put in, the more endorphins you release, the better you feel about yourself and your ability to do the work. Thus the cycle we mentioned earlier.

For example, I exercise six days a week. If I can't exercise for some reason, I park farther away from the office and walk or take the stairs to get as much activity in as possible. I don't have much time to cook during the week, so I use Sunday as my food prep day. On that one day, I prepare healthy meals to eat throughout the week. Far too many people claim they don't have time to prepare healthy food, but it can be done with just a little intentional effort! What we put into our bodies, what we drink and what we do (exercise), has the ability to make a profound impact not only on our overall lifelong health but also on our energy level and mood on a daily basis.

Another important healthy lifestyle rhythm I follow is taking a brief Sabbath from work each week and a few days in a row throughout the year. A Sabbath is simply a day to rest. After working with thirty clients weekly, following up with administrative duties, and running the business side of the practice, it's important for me to have some down time where my mind, body, and soul can be at rest.

I realized quickly after embarking on my profession that if I don't get adequate rest, which includes seven to eight hours of sleep each night and a day off each week, I won't be of any help to my clients. Perhaps in some professions, people can zone out at work and get on Facebook or ESPN from time to time to relax, but that won't really cut it in the counseling office. I look at every interaction with clients as something sacred, whereby everything in me is quieted so I can hear and see everything that is going on in them. I might be the only person in their day or even week that truly hears and sees them, so I take this job rather seriously. So, in order to offer as much focus to my last client of the week as I do to my first, I need to keep a sustainable pace throughout the week. That means I try to turn off the computer and have a pretty low-profile social schedule during the week. I try to sleep well, eat well, start my day with exercise, and daily time with God before I ever step foot into the counseling office.

I've also learned to be with mostly tier one people (see Happiness Now Questions in previous chapter) during my free time on the weekends. I've learned to surround myself with healthy, life-giving people and do things that fill me up, like spending time with friends, playing with my little nephews, serving with a local non-profit, traveling, or going to church. I get away at least once a quarter for travel so I can unplug and find a new place to explore. Detaching from work and traveling is my own type of therapy where I learn from other cultures and more about myself in the process. It might not be a super glamorous lifestyle, but it works for me. I encourage you to consider your life and the lifestyle patterns you've implemented. Which ones do you think are sustainable and life-giving? Which ones do you think are less helpful?

What it all comes down to is your willingness to make wise decisions and then follow through. Truth be told, so much of our happiness comes down to those basic disciplines. Do you want to be healthier and happier? Get intentional about creating your own systems that work for you—then follow through *consistently*. Look for solutions, not excuses. Instead of saying you have no time, figure out how to use the time you have to get what you need to perform at your best. It may take some trial and error to get it right for you, but you can do this!

ANTHONY'S OUTLOOK: PHYSICAL MATTERS

So many careers require long hours and a lot more physical activity than we realize. Many require physical motion as part of your duties. Many of the amazing CEOs and Key Executives I coach don't just sit behind a desk. They're constantly in motion from meeting to meeting, from one location to another. There's so much movement and activity that it literally takes a physical toll on all of us. Entrepreneurs are no exception. If anything, they're on the go more than most, constantly in search of more business. It all requires physical strength and stamina to juggle all the responsibilities— personal, family, career, church, community, and everything else. Quite simply, it can literally, physically wear us out.

Simply having enough energy to stagger home every night to your family doesn't work. Soon your family life will suffer, which will cause your work life to suffer, and vice versa. It begins with what we put into our bodies for fuel.

During my senior year in high school, I played the best game of football in my life. I took a hand off and headed for the end zone. With all the fans screaming, I raced toward the end zone when an opposing player caught me from behind just a few yards away from scoring a big touchdown. At first I couldn't figure it out. I should have been able to turn on the energy burst and outrun anyone on that field, but then it hit me. My pre-game meal had been a Big Mac with large fries and a soft drink from McDonald's. No wonder I was cramping up throughout the game! It was a terrible thing to do to my body right before the *Friday Night Lights* experience, but so many of us do the same thing to ourselves before the big meeting, big presentation, or big business opportunity. Then we lack the energy to finish the day strong and wonder why.

Another critical piece of ensuring we have the energy to position ourselves for happiness is getting adequate and consistent rest. I recently heard Shawn Stevenson of The Model Health Show (as I listened on the treadmill), discuss research about what he called *money sleep*—sleeping consistently each night between the hours of ten and two. According to Shawn, a person who does that consistently could probably outlast the person who gets eight hours but has an inconsistent sleeping pattern.

I try for a consistent bedtime. Candidly, I don't always achieve it, but I average sleeping in the 10:30 pm to 3:30 am window. My scheduled wake time varies from 3:30 to 4:30 a.m. depending on whether or not I have a workout scheduled. I'm also a big believer in taking twenty to thirty minute power naps—if I can get one in during a normal day. With the way my DNA is wired, I can grab thirty minutes and be re-energized. That may not work for everyone in every situation, but it's a valuable tool in my physical energy toolkit.

Along with eating well and getting focused rest, I work out an average of seven hours a week. Now, I don't go every day, but it works out to about an hour a day average for me—cardio and strength conditioning. I don't claim to be an expert on such things, but I can fully attest to the beneficial daily results I experience as a result of my consistent commitment to working out.

Another important piece of the physical coordinate to me is being intentional about unplugging to rest and recharge. It helps to know how you are wired so you can lean into activities that restore your energy. For example, my wife is a little more introverted than I am. While engaging with people energizes me, engaging with people drains her. Sitting still drains me; in fact, I view working out as a form of relaxation. My wife works out consistently, but prefers smooth jazz and a hot bath for relaxation. It works for her, but it would drive me nuts if I did it too often! But that's ok. Each of us is unique. The important thing is that we schedule time to unplug doing something—or nothing—to make sure we recharge.

If not, we could easily end up caught up in the relentless pursuit of the American Dream. We live in a capitalistic culture; for the most part, that's a good thing. Capitalism drives our infrastructure. But it doesn't have to own you.

We professionals spend about two thirds of our time (if not more) engaged in work and career efforts. Consequently, much of our happiness is connected to our work and career environments because we spend so much time there. Yet we still spend more time trying to make more money thinking money will solve all our problems. We don't take the time to pull over and refuel or recharge. And when we do, it's just more work in disguise.

I was once on a call with a mastermind group where a successful woman shared that her life was completely out of balance. "But you're all going to be so proud of me," she told us. "I've taken two and a half days off since we started talking three months ago!"

Stunned, I followed with a question: "Are you including weekends in the number?"

"Yes! I can't find room not to work because of the work I do." She went on to give some details about the many events swirling around her calendar then concluded with admitting she needed to find some time for herself and her family. "But, you know what I do to unplug? I volunteer more. I just found two more boards to serve on."

Before we judge too harshly, so many of us get caught up in the storm of capitalism. Rather than pursuing a values-driven capitalism, we get swept away by greed and then wonder why we aren't happier.

ANTHONY'S OUTLOOK: YOUR PHYSICAL LOCATION

Beyond your physical health habits, your physical surroundings dramatically shape your potential for happiness. Your daily physical environment—where you are, who you are with, and what you experience—can dramatically affect your physical health and, in turn, your happiness.

For example, people often stay in work or home environments that are paralyzing, cancerous, and downright destructive over the long-term. But they don't see the need to get out—like a frog swimming in water that doesn't realize the danger from the flames below until it's too late. Your physical location can be toxic and we all tend to absorb the culture around us. So, if your work environment is pessimistic, you'll tend to gradually become more negative in your thinking. On the other hand, if your physical work location and the work culture both affirm positive growth and affirm your value, you'll tend to be more productive and engaged.

Think about people living in poverty, something I can relate to first-hand. I remember being told, "Anthony, if you hang around nine broke people, you are destined to be number ten." Most people in my world carried a poverty mindset that surrounded us all in our physical location. The hopeless mentality that existed there, not to mention potential harm from drugs, prostitution, and crime, influenced the decisions people made about future options. If people who've chosen a miserable status quo surround you, you may have to physically put yourself in a different environment that will empower you to thrive.

I grew up surrounded by all of it. As a kid, I saw a man get stabbed and watched him stumble to a nearby apartment to call an ambulance, then sit on the stairwell only to bleed while waiting. That environment influenced my thinking and I could have easily chosen to stay put, but made the decision to change my physical and mental real estate. I chose to change locations to a more positive place. I changed my mental and physical location to a place that positively impacted my life instead of a place that held me back from finding happiness in this life.

It's not that all people in poverty-stricken communities lack the intelligence to get out. For many, it's simply the only environment they know. But a similar thing happens in the workplace. Young professionals graduate college and go into a work environment that's toxic without realizing it. After all, for many it's their first job. They don't realize that there is life outside of the physical space they live and work in every day.

Thus, they also don't stop to consider what they can do to improve their work and life environments.

Regardless of the environment you came from or find yourself in now, you can still choose happiness with proper training, but being in an intentionally destructive environment makes it far more difficult to do. If you find yourself in a toxic environment, will you stay in the same place or will you move to a physical—and mental—location that positions you to live a more fulfilling life? And remember, *you* may be the one creating the toxic environment. The solution may be to change your own attitude about your present circumstances rather than run somewhere else— and take the problem with you.

EMILY'S OUTLOOK: CASE STUDY

One health-conscious client was a collegiate athlete, but after graduating and moving forward in her career, she let her health go to the wayside. She reached and exceeded what was expected of her in the first quarter in her new role. And yet she was miserable. When I first spoke to her, she hadn't slept for a full seven or eight hours in at least six months. She had no social life and the only exercise she got was walking from her hotel to the taxi each day.

She had already gained fifteen pounds that year, after gaining twenty pounds the year before. She was supposedly succeeding by most definitions of the word, but she couldn't even fit into her own clothes and she didn't have time to buy new clothes. Finally, she decided she just couldn't live like that anymore. She had a family history of diabetes, as well, so having a healthy diet and exercise was not only vital to her self-image, but essential to her overall health. We talked about the importance of sleep hygiene (healthy sleep habits). She began trying to get at least six hours each night by limiting her computer and TV use to end an hour before bedtime.

She rearranged her work schedule so she was traveling for work in similar time zones as much as possible. She still had to travel between London and Shanghai, but her employers worked with her to create a more efficient travel schedule and used video meetings when possible. We discussed simple ways to exercise more, like walking from one terminal to the next at the airport or walking to the hotel instead of taking the taxi when her meetings were close. She aimed to have at least thirty minutes of exercise three times a week and her energy level started to increase significantly. She started eating healthier options and avoided those late-night sugary foods she often craved when sleep deprived. She replaced soft drinks with green tea, and binge-watching television with reading. She developed an entirely new outlook on life by intentionally creating a better system for physical health that worked for her.

We all get busy, but being too busy for self-care will lead us to unfulfilling places, especially when experiencing intense stress. When we're too busy to exercise is exactly when we will get the most benefit from doing it. Because we are dynamic individuals, our stress doesn't simply stay at bay. It either increases or decreases over time. And we can control it.

The same is true for emotions, too. When everything goes crazy, it's human nature to deem self-care a luxury and wait until the storm passes. By implementing healthy habits you can have the buoyancy to not only survive the storm but to thrive through it. If your schedule is "crazy busy" you are too busy NOT to implement healthy habits!

JUST DO IT

Doing the right thing requires stamina. Life is hard, but it's so worth it. Stamina is directly responsible for helping you to get through the storms you face in life. You can create new paths that allow you to get from here to where you want to go. How you currently take care of your body (diet, exercise, and sleep), and your physical location are all indicators we use to determine the status of happiness in the physical coordinate of your *Happiness Map*.

This is all part of the physical system you need to develop catered to who you are. You have to use your own system in order to elicit what works best for you. It's a process of learning how you're wired, then leaning into it. If you need to listen to smooth jazz to relax, then do it. If you need to hang out with friends, then do it. If you need to go to a weight room in order to physically exercise, then do it. Find what works best for you--then do it.

THE BOTTOM LINE

- Your physical health determines your energy levels and your capacity to sustain success.
- Regular physical exercise and adequate, consistent rest don't just build muscle; they build your brain and prepare you to perform at your best.
- All it takes is 20 minutes of focused, intense, and effective exercise every day to give yourself a healthy happiness boost.
- Sometimes the solution is to change your own attitude about your present circumstances rather than run somewhere else and take the problem with you.
- If people who surround you have chosen a miserable status quo, you may have to physically put yourself in a different environment that will empower you to thrive.

HAPPINESS NOW QUESTIONS

Destination: Where Do I Want to Go?

1. What are my long-term physical goals? This could include completing a half marathon by age 50, maintaining your goal weight, or having low cholesterol and blood sugar at your yearly doctor visits. Be creative and be sure to write down a variety of "big picture" physical goals you'd like to accomplish.

   _____

   _____

2. Who's someone who is ten to twenty years my senior whose already met and exceeded some of these goals?

   _____

   _____

3. How long do I want to live? What kind of quality of life do I want to have as I age?

   _____

   _____

Location: Where am I Now?

1. Am I eating, sleeping, exercising, and behaving in a manner that is healthy and sustainable?

    _____

    _____

2. What would a doctor or nutritionist say if they were to see my daily food and exercise log?

    _____

    _____

3. If not, what are the top two to three areas that need the most attention? What are the barriers to me improving each area?

    _____

    _____

Realization: What do I Need to Change to Close the Gap?

1. What are some realistic goals that I can implement for the next thirty to sixty days?

   _____

   _____

   a. Eating:
   b. Exercising:
   c. Sleeping:
   d. Unplugging:

2. Overeaters Anonymous has an acronym to help members when tempted to overeat called HALT (Am I Hungry, Angry, Lonely, or Tired?) By asking themselves this question, they learn to stop themselves from eating or drinking when they need to attend to their true emotional need in the moment. Do I ever use food or drinks to self medicate when stressed, tired, lonely, or angry? If so, what can I do instead to tend to my real need—my heart hunger, not my head hunger.

   _____

   _____

3. Often, New Year's Resolutions don't work because people create unrealistic expectations, timelines, and outcomes for themselves. After not meeting their unobtainable goal after the first week, they trash the plan entirely. They might have wonderful intentions, but their execution is set up for failure. As I think of unhealthy habits in my life, what are one or two small steps that I can take in each area to reach my overall goal?

_____

_____

4. What is my "self talk" when I don't reach my goals? Write them down as you go throughout your week. When you make unwise food, sleep, or exercise decisions, note what you say to yourself about yourself. Oftentimes, the negative scripts in our head will mess us up and get us off track far more than the initial poor choice ever did!

_____

_____

We've included some scripts often shared in counseling sessions and encourage you to circle the ones that coincide with what you wrote down in your week of observations. See our responses to some below and be sure to create your own responses to the additional comments as well as the scripts you add to the list in the space below:

- **Negative:** I'm too tired to exercise after work because work drains everything out of me! Once I get a new job, I'll be more energized and I'll actually want to work out.
- **Positive:** I might be too tired because my work takes a lot out of me, but I bet I could find something fun that provides physical exercise and also gives me something to look forward to do after work. Maybe I can join a rec league or walk with a friend after work. Since my job is so draining, I need to be responsible and proactive in finding activities that fill me back up during the hours I'm away from work.
- **Negative:** I don't feel good about myself, so what's the point of taking care of my body? If I looked like my attractive friends and co-workers, I would totally work out and eat well but there's not point for me. It won't work for me like it does for them.
- **Positive:** I might be a bit overweight and out of shape but my weight doesn't determine my worth. Some people might be more fit than me, because of good genes and luck, but I have to put some sweat equity into looking better. This might feel unfair but a lot of

life is unfair. Once I realize that, I can accept it and do something about it. I'm going to start doing something about it today by going to the gym and bringing meals from home instead of eating out for lunch and dinner.

- **Negative:** I've tried to eat well but I went on vacation and never got back on track. I've had a hard time following through, so why try again now?
- **Positive:**
- **Negative:** No one in my family takes time off. We are all running from work, to practices, and to other commitments. We never sit down to actually read, talk, or be still. I can appreciate the benefits, but when everyone else isn't being healthy, I don't feel compelled to do anything differently.
- **Positive:**

Acceleration: How Can I Best Move Forward Consistently?

1. What can I immediately change about myself that would ultimately impact my current health and healthy lifestyle?

_____

_____

2. Although I cannot fully own others' healthy life decisions, what can I do to positively influence health patterns in the lives of my immediate family members or friends?

_____

_____

3. What three things will I do in the next ninety days consistently to alter the trajectory of my family's ability to rest and recharge outside of work and school hours?

_____

_____

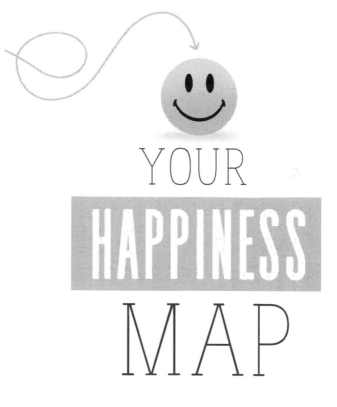

YOUR
HAPPINESS
MAP

Remember: This book will *not* make you happy. By now, it should be clear that **YOU are the key to your own happiness.** That truth gives you tremendous power—and responsibility. Focusing on the Happiness Coordinates— Financial, Family, Community, and Physical, will give direction while you continue your journey toward happiness. You also know how to apply the 4 Fulfillment Factors— Destination, Location, Realization, and Acceleration. Using these in conjunction with your coordinates will ensure you know where you're going, how you're going to get there, and what you need to do to reach your destination.

Having a prestigious education, an impressive salary or title, and a healthy family are all wonderful goals, but they are not the answer to finding happiness. **Happiness comes as a byproduct of aligning your coordinates with your purpose.** As you've read from our personal stories and examples, this isn't an easy process. Pursuing your purpose and making sure your coordinates are aligned can be a taxing effort. But the harsh reality is that not doing so can lead to downright misery.

Want to be happy? Don't stay stuck where you are. Don't continue drifting into someone else's lane (dream of what should be). Don't chase a corrupted version of the American Dream only to find out it was an unsatisfying myth. Use your story, use your pain, use your past to move forward. Quit comparing your internal thoughts and feelings with the way other people appear externally. Stop wishing your past looked different. Don't try to present an ideal version of the life you wish you had. Find happiness in the life, in the family, in the present realities you have now. Spend more time on cultivating your character than managing your image.

In her memoir *Fight Back With Joy*, Margaret Feinburg tells of her battle with cancer, from diagnosis to remission, and how she learned to experience joy most fully when most people would have felt defeated and despondent:

Create your own permission slip for joy. Write three words: Accept. Adapt. Depend. Carry this permission slip with you. Tell your friends you're working on becoming more content/ more joyful. Take a nap. Live with a messy house for a time. Order takeout. File an extension on your taxes. Stare out the window. Linger in the company of a friend. Breathe in the fullness of life. Use those words to fight back with joy.[51]

Happiness is worth fighting for because you are worth fighting for! You now have permission to be happy, regardless of your past or present realities. Whatever season of life you're going through, we encourage you to use the contents of this book to cultivate what is most life-giving and rewarding. Choose the path that leads to happiness. Choose your purpose. Enable your Life GPS. Then align your 4 Happiness Coordinates by applying the 4 Fulfillment

Factors consistently. Imagine the impact in your life and on the generations to follow as you pass along these tools to your children, neighbors, colleagues, and community. Your commitment to cultivate happiness in your life now will allow you to pass down a map for happiness to future generations. What a gift!

Disappointment, depression, financial crisis, unmet desires, shattered dreams, and life transitions all have a way of kicking the wind out of you. They can leave you without any extra energy to look for silver linings. Sadness can be even more pronounced when it happens during what we think should be a happy season of life. Even in the sadness, the emptiness, or the loneliness, *you have a choice*—we all do. We can choose to focus on what we think is lacking and lose ourselves in the endless comparison game, or we can do something far more original and difficult but much more fulfilling. We can apply the 4 x 4 Happiness Model each day, putting one foot in front of the other until, sometimes with little fanfare, we realize we're happier and more fulfilled in work and life than ever before. We encourage you to take this challenge for the next 90 days and we assure you, you'll be glad you did!

Visit TheHappinessMapBook.com to retake the assessment now that you've completed the book.

Check your happiness levels and discover more about how we can help you achieve fulfillment in work and life. We can't wait to hear your own Happiness Map success story and help you share it with others!

ENDNOTES

1 Todd B. Kashdan, "The Problem with Happiness," *Psychology Today*, (blog), September 29, 2010, www.psychologytoday.com/blog/curious/201009/the-problem-happiness.

2 *Merriam Webster Dictionary, s.v.* "happy," https://www.merriam-webster.com/dictionary/happy

3 *Ibid.*

4 Jenny Joseph, "When I Am Old," in *Barbados–Poems and Poetry* http://www.barbados.org/poetry/wheniam.htm

5 United States Census Bureau. "Income, Poverty and Health Insurance Coverage in the United States: 2013." News release. https://www.census.gov/newsroom/press-releases/2014/cb14-169.html

6 Joseph LaLonde, "Your Past Doesn't Define You. It Helps Shape You", (blog) September 6, 2013, http://www.jmlalonde.com/your-past-doesnt-define-you-it-helps-shape you/.

7 Jim Loehr and Tony Scwartz, *The Power of Full Engagement*, (New York: Free Press, 2005).

8 Sonja Lyubomirsky, *The How of Happiness: A New Approach to Getting the Life You Want* (New York: Penguin Books, 2008).

9 Jonathan Haidt, *The Happiness Hypothesis* (New York: Basic Books, 2006).

10 Tony Dungy and Nathan Whitaker, *Quiet Strength: the Principles, Practices, & Priorities of a Winning Life* (Carol Stream: Tyndale House Publishers, 2007).

11 David Brooks, *The Road to Character* (New York: Random House, 2015).

12 Carolyn M. Brown, "Tyler Perry On How To Find Success After Failure," *Black Enterprise* (blog) November 25, 2014, http://www.blackenterprise.com/small-business/tyler-perry-on-finding-success-after-failure/.

13 Neil Pasricha, "The Happiness Equation: Want Nothing + Do Anything = Have Everything" (New York: G.P. Putnams Sons, 2016).

14 Edward L. Deci, Veronika Huta, and Richard M. Ryan, "Living Well: A Self-Determination Theory Perspective on Eudaimonia," *Journal of Happiness Studies* 9, no.1 (2008) : 139-170.

15 Bill Blankschaen, *A Story Worth Telling: Your Field Guide to Living an Authentic Life* (Nashville: Abingdon Press, 2015).

16 Justin Bibb and Steven Bosacker, "Most City Employees in U.S. Not Engaged," *Gallup News* (blog), May 16, 2017, www.gallup.com/opinion/gallup/210707/city-employees-not-engaged.aspx.

17 Susie Poppick, "The Only 3 Things You Need to Know About Money's Effect on Happiness," *Money* (blog), January 28, 2015, time.com/money/3680465/happiness-and-money-study/.

18 Maia Szalavitz, "Why the Rich Are Less Ethical: They See Greed as Good." *Time* (blog), February 28, 2012, healthland.time.com/2012/02/28/why-the-rich-are-less-ethical-they-see-greed-as-good/.

19 Sierra Black, "Money CAN Buy Your Happiness!," *Get Rich Slowly* (blog), October 5, 2016, http://www.getrichslowly.org/blog/2010/08/19/money-can-buy-you-happiness/

20 Mark Fahey, "Money Can Buy Happiness, But Only to a Point," *CNBC* (blog), December 14, 2015 (11:30 a.m.), https://www.cnbc.com/2015/12/14/money-can-buy-happiness-but-only-to-a-point.html

21 Brady Josephson, "Want To Be Happier? Give More. Give Better", HuffPost (blog), January 21, 2015, (12:45 p.m.), http://www.huffingtonpost.com/brady-josephson/want-to-be-happier-give-m_b_6175358.html

22 Minda Zetlin, "When Trouble at Home Becomes Trouble in the Office," *Inc.* (blog), July 8, 2013, https://www.inc.com/minda-zetlin/employee-facing-personal-problems-heres-what-to-do.html

23 Owen Bowcott, "Relationship Breakdowns Have Negative Impact on Business Productivity," The Guardian (blog), November 25, 2014, (7:01 p.m.), https://www.theguardian.com/

lifeandstyle/2014/nov/26/relationship-breakdowns-business-productivity-employees-divorce-separation

24 Alison Aughinbaugh, Omar Robles, and Hugette Sun,"Marriage and Divorce: Patterns by Gender, Race, and Educational Attainment," *Monthly Labor Review*, October 2013, https://doi.org/10.21916/mlr.2013.32.

25 Meg Murphy, "Why Millennials Refuse to Get Married," *NowUKnow* (blog), August 29, 2017, http://www.bentley.edu/impact/articles/nowuknow-why-millennials-refuse-get-married.

26 Suniya S. Luthar, Ph.d., "The Problem With Rich Kids," *Psychology Today*, (blog), November 5, 2013, www.psychologytoday.com/articles/201311/the-problem-rich-kids.

27 MetroLyrics, *Parents Just Don't Understand,* http://www.metrolyrics.com/parents-just-dont-understand-w-dj-jazzy-jeff-lyrics-will-smith.html

28 Michael Fulwiler, "The 6 Things That Predict Divorce." *Gottman Relationship Blog* (blog), October 10, 2014, www.gottman.com/blog/the-6-things-that-predict-divorce/.

29 *Ibid.*

30 *Ibid.*

31 Ed Diener and Martin E.P. Seligman, "Very Happy People," *Psychological Science* 13, no. 1 (2002) : pg. 81-84, doi:10.1111/1467-9280.00415.

32 Claudia Wallis, The New Science of Happiness," *Time* (blog), January 9, 2005, content.time.com/time/magazine/article/ 0,9171,1015832,00.html.

33 Mary Jo Kreitzer, "Why Personal Relationships Are Important," *Taking Charge of Your Health & Wellbeing* (blog), www. takingcharge.csh.umn.edu/why-personal-relationships-are-important.

34 Jane E. Brody, "Social Interaction Is Critical for Mental and Physical Health." *The New York Times* (blog), June 12, 2017, www. nytimes.com/2017/06/12/well/live/having-friends-is-good-for-you.html?mcubz=0.

35 J. Bradley Layton, Julianne Holt-Lunstad, and Timothy B. Smith, "Social Relationships and Mortality Risk: A Meta-Analytic Review." *PLOS Medicine,* (2010), doi:10.4016/19865.01.

36 Gallup, Inc., "State of the American Workplace." *Gallup News,* www.gallup.com/reports/199961/state-american-work place-report-2017.aspx?utm_source=SOAW&utm_campaign =StateofAmericanWorkplace&utm_medium=2013SOAWreport.

37 Huang Haifang and John Helliwell, "Comparing the Happiness Effects of Real and On-Line Friends." *PLOS One* (2013), doi:10.3386/ w18690.

38 *Ibid.*

39 "Mentoring Impact." *Go to MENTOR*, www.mentoring.org/why-mentoring/mentoring-impact/. Accessed September 2, 2017.

40 John Brandon, "Why You Need a Mentor to Point Out Your Flaws--and Your Potential." *Inc.com* (blog), November 17, 2016, www.inc.com/john-brandon/why-you-need-a-mentor-to-point-out-your-flaws-and-your-potential.html.

41 Penn State, "Physical Activity Yields Feelings of Excitement, Enthusiasm." *EurekAlert!,* (blog), February 8, 2012, www.eurekalert.org/pub_releases/2012-02/ps-pay020812.php.

42 Diana Yates, "Physically Fit Kids Have Beefier Brain White Matter Than Their Less-Fit Peers." *Illinois News Bureau* (blog), August 19, 2014 (9:00 a.m.), news.illinois.edu/blog/view/6367/204540.

43 Gretchen Reynolds, "How Exercise Can Jog the Memory," *Well* (blog), May 30, 2012 (12:01 a.m.), well.blogs.nytimes.com/2012/05/30/how-exercise-can-jog-the-memory/.

44 Dr. Mercola. "What Happens in Your Body When You Exercise?" *Peak Fitness* (blog), September 20, 2013, fitness.mercola.com/sites/fitness/archive/2013/09/20/exercise-health-benefits.aspx.

45 "BDNF brain derived neurotrophic factor [Homo sapiens (Human)] - Gene - NCBI." *National Center for Biotechnology Information*, accessed September 4, 2017, www.ncbi.nlm.nih.gov/gene/627

46 MK McGovern, "The Effects of Exercise on the Brain." July 19, 2012,, serendip.brynmawr.edu/bb/neuro/neuro05/web2/mmc govern.html.

47 Gretchen Reynolds, *The First 20 Minutes: The Surprising Science of How We Can Exercise Better, Train Smarter and Live Longer,* (New York: Penguin, 2013).

48 Daily Mail Reporter, "People Who Exercise on Work Days Are Happier, Suffer Less Stress and Are More Productive." *DailyMail. com* (blog), December 16, 2008, (12:33 (a.m.), www.dailymail. co.uk/news/article-1095783/People-exercise-work-days-happier-suffer-stress-productive.html.

49 Gretchen Reynolds, "How Exercise Can Jog the Memory," *Well* (blog), May 30, 2012 (12:01 a.m.), well.blogs.nytimes. com/2012/05/30/how-exercise-can-jog-the-memory/.

50 Ira Dreyfuss and Associated Press, "Exercise Found as Effective as Antidepressant Zoloft," *Los Angeles Times* (blog), October 1, 2000, articles.latimes.com/2000/oct/01/news/mn-29539

51 Margaret Feinberg, *Fight Back with Joy: celebrate more. Regret less. Stare down your greatest fears* (Brentwood: Worthy Publishing, 2015).

73436085R00148